Contents

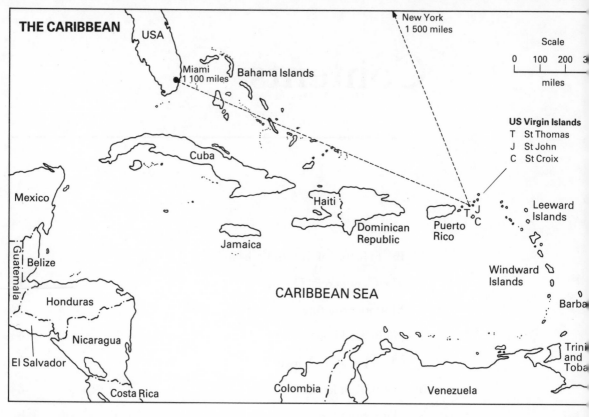

THE CARIBBEAN

New York
1 500 miles

Scale

0   100   200   3

miles

USA

Miami
1 100 miles

Bahama Islands

Cuba

Mexico

Haiti

Dominican
Republic

Jamaica

Puerto
Rico

US Virgin Islands
T   St Thomas
J   St John
C   St Croix

Leeward
Islands

Windward
Islands

Barba

CARIBBEAN SEA

Guatemala

Belize

Honduras

Nicaragua

El Salvador

Costa Rica

Colombia

Venezuela

Trini
and
Toba

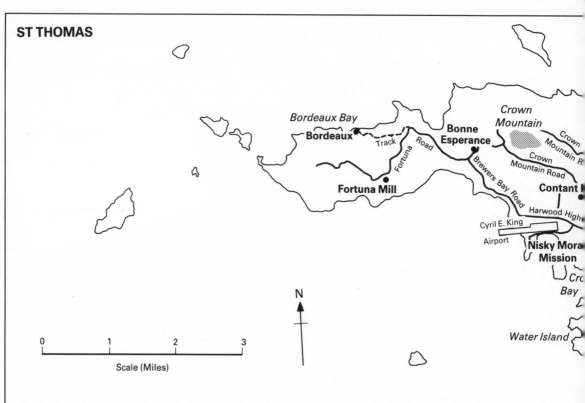

ST THOMAS

Bordeaux Bay

Bordeaux

*Crown
Mountain*

**Bonne
Esperance**

Track

Fortuna Road

Crown

Mountain R

Crown
Mountain Road

Brewers Bay Road

Contant

Fortuna Mill

Harwood High

Cyril E. King

Airport

**Nisky Mora
Mission**

Cro

Bay

Water Island

N

0   1   2   3

Scale (Miles)

Historic Buildings of St Thomas and St John

Frederik C. Gjessing and William P. MacLean

MACMILLAN
CARIBBEAN

First published 1987

Published by *Macmillan Publishers Ltd*
London and Basingstoke
*Associated companies and representatives in Accra,
Auckland, Delhi, Dublin, Gaborone, Hamburg, Harare,
Hong Kong, Kuala Lumpur, Lagos, Manzini, Melbourne,
Mexico City, Nairobi, New York, Singapore, Tokyo*

British Library Cataloguing in Publication Data
Gjessing, Frederik C.
    Historic buildings of St Thomas and St John.
    1. Historic buildings — Virgin Islands of
    the United States — Guide-books
    I. Title II. MacLean, William P. *1943—*
    917.297'2204   F2136.2

ISBN 0−333−37382−0

Printed in Hong Kong

Cover picture: Charlotte Amalie and St Thomas harbor.
The Reformed Church is clearly visible in the left
foreground. Reproduced from a lithograph by Baerentzen.

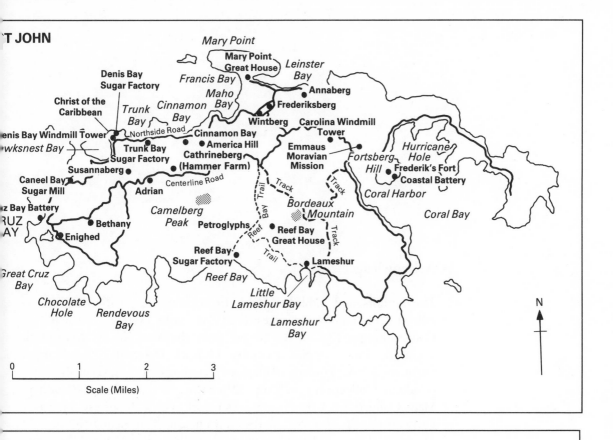

ST JOHN

Mary Point

Mary Point Great House

Leinster Bay

Francis Bay

Maho Bay

Annaberg

Denis Bay Sugar Factory

Frederiksberg

Cinnamon Bay

Christ of the Caribbean

Wintberg

Carolina Windmill Tower

Trunk Bay

Denis Bay Windmill Tower

Northside Road

Cinnamon Bay

Hurricane Hole

Hawksnest Bay

Trunk Bay Sugar Factory

America Hill

Emmaus Moravian Mission

Fortsberg Hill

Frederik's Fort Coastal Battery

Cathrineberg (Hammer Farm)

Caneel Bay Sugar Mill

Susannaberg

Centerline Road

Track

Coral Harbor

Cruz Bay Battery

Adrian

Track

Bordeaux Mountain

Coral Bay

CRUZ BAY

Camelberg Peak

Petroglyphs

Reef Bay Trail

Reef Bay Great House

Bethany

Enighed

Track

Great Cruz Bay

Reef Bay Sugar Factory

Trail

Lameshur

Chocolate Hole

Rendevous Bay

Reef Bay

Little Lameshur Bay

Lameshur Bay

0   1   2   3

Scale (Miles)

N

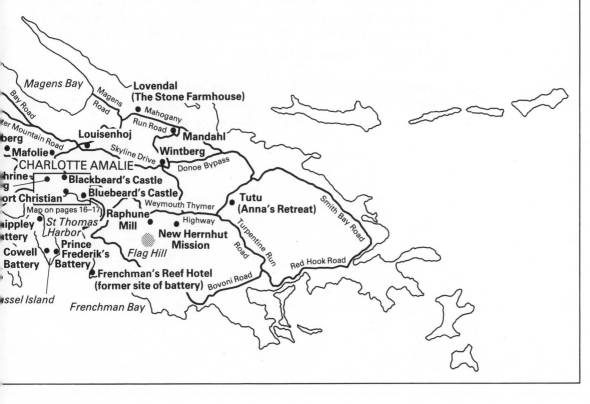

Magens Bay

Lovendal (The Stone Farmhouse)

Bay Road

Magens Road

Mahogany Run Road

Louisenhoj

Mandahl

Mountain Road

Wintberg

berg

Mafolie

Skyline Drive

CHARLOTTE AMALIE

Donoe Bypass

shrine

Blackbeard's Castle

Tutu (Anna's Retreat)

ort Christian

Bluebeard's Castle

Smith Bay Road

Map on pages 16–17

Weymouth Thymer

Raphune Mill

hippley attery

St Thomas Harbor

Highway

Turpentine Run Road

New Herrnhut Mission

Cowell Battery

Prince Frederik's Battery

Flag Hill

Red Hook Road

Frenchman's Reef Hotel (former site of battery)

Bovoni Road

ssel Island

Frenchman Bay

Acknowledgements

The authors and publishers wish to acknowledge, with thanks, the following photographic sources: Enid Baa Public Library, Van Scholten Collection, pp 12, 14, 18 (insert from the Van Keulen Map of St Thomas); Handel og Søfartsmuseet, Elinsore, Denmark p10; Library of Congress USA, Historic American Buildings Survey, Danish Royal Academy Collection pp 25 top, 29 centre, 68 top, 70 top; Rigarkivet Map Collection, Copenhagen, Denmark pp 4 (courtesy of Isidor Paeiwonsky, St Thomas), 8 (insert from the Van Keulen Map of St Thomas), 33 top, 34 top (courtesy of the Enid Baa Public Library, St Thomas), 34 bottom, 37 top, 38, 40, 44. All other photographs are by courtesy of the authors. The cover picture is a lithograph by Baerentzen of Charlotte Amalie and St Thomas Harbor.

The publishers have made every effort to trace the copyright holders, but if they have inadvertently overlooked any, they will be pleased to make the necessary arrangements at the first opportunity.

1 Brief History of the Virgin Islands

There are two basically different ways of writing history. The scholarly approach seeks to answer questions of cause and effect which are the deep concern of a relatively small group of experts. Our purpose here is quite different. History does have considerable entertainment value for the general reader. The broad sweep of history excites most intellects, and almost everyone's imagination can be captivated by historical anecdotes, which is why historical novels, plays, movies, and so forth are successful. We hope to both inform and entertain with the following popular history of St Thomas and St John. Our approach is to talk about the old buildings found on these islands, because this is how an interest in history is often aroused.

Our brief synopsis of Virgin Islands history which follows is a skeleton on which the reader is invited to hang flesh and guts through additional reading — some titles are recommended in the bibliography. It is also the briefest context necessary for imagining the communities which produced the historic buildings we describe and illustrate.

Columbus discovered the Virgin Islands in 1493, on his second voyage. He named the fertile and well-populated island first sighted Santa Cruz. The expedition's landing at Salt River was soon followed by an attack from Carib Indians, the first hostilities experienced by Columbus. The ships left immediately, sailing towards the land on the horizon to the north, where they anchored at dusk. The following morning he explored what turned out to be an archipelago of mountainous islands, cays, and banks separated by narrow bodies of water. Their great number, and perhaps their numerous mammiform hills — a type of imagery seldom wasted on nautical men — inspired Columbus to name these islands Las Islas Vírgenes, in honor of St Ursula and her army of 11,000 virgins. He was not impressed by the Virgins, which he described as barren, and the fleet sailed west that same day, to explore Puerto Rico.

Exploring, colonizing, exploiting, and Christianizing the Greater Antilles, the American continents, and the Philippine Islands kept Spain busy during the sixteenth century, leaving no resources for the Lesser

Antilles and other peripheral areas to be colonized. Other than briefly exploiting the copper deposits on Virgin Gorda and making a few raids on the Carib Indians of St Croix, the Spanish colonists ignored the Virgin Islands. Their sheltered bays were left unguarded, available for the use of ships of other nations. These included traders, freebooters, and the naval heros of Elizabethan England — John Hawkins, Francis Drake, and the Earl of Cumberland — whom the Spaniards, of course, considered to be pirates. French captains and corsairs also enriched themselves and their government by raids on the Spanish Caribbean colonies and galleons.

During the sixteenth century, trading and raiding by the French and English established that Spain lacked the power to enforce its claim to the entire Caribbean. In the seventeenth century, the Dutch, French, and English colonized the smaller islands and parts of larger islands not settled by the Spanish. The Stuart kings issued vague and generous letters of patent on islands of the Lesser Antilles to English noblemen, and Dutch and French companies were authorized by their governments to claim possession of Caribbean lands. New waves of settlement resulted. In the Virgins, the first resident Europeans were Dutch and English. They had become established on St Croix by 1625. The Dutch settled Tortola in 1648.

St Thomas and St John were still unsettled and essentially ownerless in the 1660s. While unattractive for plantation agriculture, due to the mountainous terrain, they had some timber, a little water, and excellent harbors. The greatest deterrent to their colonization was proximity to the Spanish in Puerto Rico. Traders from the United Kingdom of Denmark and Norway (henceforth referred to as Denmark-Norway) enjoyed some success in the Caribbean in the mid-seventeenth century, and they started to advocate the establishment of a colony as early as 1652. In 1665, a group of Copenhagen merchants formed the first Danish West India Company to pursue this objective. With the government's permission, it sent out a small expeditionary force which, in 1666, took possession of St Thomas. There appears to have been as many as 50 people of various European nationalities on St Thomas when the expedition arrived, but there is some confusion on this point.

The late seventeenth century was a difficult time for small settlements in the West Indies. The European war of England against Holland and France had spread to the Caribbean and the legalized piracy of the previous century was again in full force. In 1666 the small Dutch colony on Tortola was driven out by a band of buccaneers who claimed to be English. The refugees sought protection with the neutral Danes of St Thomas, where they were welcomed because additional manpower was needed. This apparent blessing unfortunately proved otherwise for the new colony, because it provided a justification for freebooters of all the warring nations to raid. They ostensibly came to capture the refugees and to free their own and other nationals, but the result was that they helped themselves to supplies and equipment, including a ship, which the Danes could not defend. The decimation of their numbers, deprivation, and lack of supplies forced the colonists to abandon St Thomas in 1668 and return to Denmark.

The first Danish expedition had been a failure, but the reports of its struggles and findings stirred the imagination of others, and in 1671 a new West India Company was chartered. Like the first, it was a private company, but it was much better capitalized and counted among its stockholders the King and several other members of the royal family. Unlike the first, this company received direct support from the government, in the form of a naval squadron and personnel. In addition, Denmark had cemented its diplomatic relations with Holland and had entered into an alliance and commercial agreement with England, which augured well for a new colony.

The second Danish expedition reached St Thomas in 1672. Its governor was Jorgen Iversen, who was well acquainted with the West Indies. He had lived for 14 years in the British colony of St Kitts, where he had risen from indentured servant to full partner and West Indian agent of a Dutch trading concern. He had returned to Denmark in 1665 a wealthy man.

Like the first, the second group of colonizers suffered an alarming mortality rate during the passage from Europe and the early months of settlement. As in 1666, they were soon joined by dispossessed planters from other islands, who this time were allowed to remain in peace. The arrival of the Danes on St Thomas did, however, require some reaction. Sir Charles Wheeler, Governor of the English Leeward Islands, sought to deny the Danes the right to any of the Virgin Islands, as did the Spanish governor of Puerto Rico. These protestations were settled by diplomatic means. Charles II of England was persuaded to declare the Danes the rightful occupants of St Thomas, probably to deny the island to Spain, and to replace Wheeler with Sir William Stapleton. The King of England's statement was then presented to the Spanish court, and their objections dwindled.

Immediately after the Danes landed, work commenced on a fort, land clearing, road building, and the construction of shelters. The work was pushed relentlessly by Governor Iversen, who not only used Company employees, but also drafted planters and their slaves for these labors. His despotic ways alienated many and the colony became known in Denmark as 'the charnel house ruled by a tyrant'. This reputation made it difficult to find immigrants. When Iversen was relieved at his own request in 1680, there were only 156 whites and 175 blacks on St Thomas. He left a completed Fort Christian, also known as Christians Fort (which had repelled a French attack in 1678), 50 surveyed plantations (46 of which were occupied), and an east-west road through the island. Cargos of sugar, cotton, tobacco, and other produce had been sent home and income was increasing. The West India Company was not yet operating at a profit, but under Iversen its prospects continued to improve considerably.

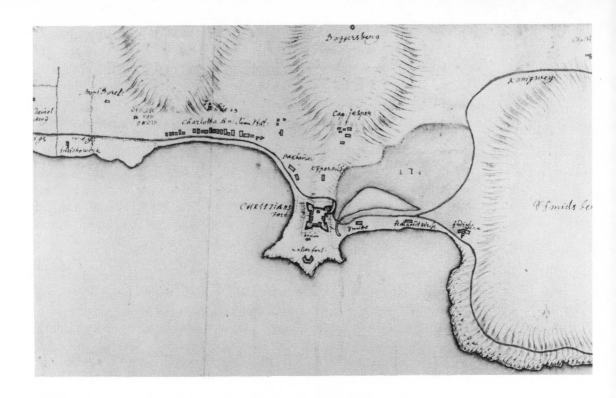

Seventeenth century Danish map of St Thomas harbor.

The following three governorships lasted only six years, during which the personal ambition and greed of the governors undid much of Jorgen Iversen's work, bringing the Company near to bankruptcy, and the St Thomas colony close to extinction. The infamous Esmit brothers were illegally and openly trading with freebooters and even allowing pirates to sail under the Danish flag. St Thomas became known as a pirate's den. Governor Adolph Esmit confiscated property for his personal use, known to have been robbed from English citizens, causing Sir William Stapleton to complain to the British Government, which, in turn, presented the Danish king with an ultimatum demanding restitution and Esmit's arrest.

This ultimatum caused considerable consternation in Denmark, where the government was unaware of Esmit's crimes. With all the speed possible in the seventeenth century, the West India Company sent out a new governor, Gabriel Milan, with instructions to return Adolph Esmit to Denmark aboard the naval ship *Fortuna*. Milan ignored these orders and refused to supply a cargo for the *Fortuna*, detaining it for more than six months. The captain finally departed against Milan's orders and without cargo or Aldolph Esmit.

The disturbing news of Governor Milan's mismanagement caused the West India Company to petition the Danish Government to send the *Fortuna* back to St Thomas with a commissioner authorized to hold hearings. Esmit was to be returned to Denmark for trial, as was Milan, if a case could be made against him. Milan was to be relieved and an acting-governor appointed.

By the time the *Fortuna* reached St Thomas, the situation had gone from bad to worse. Governor Milan tried to coerce the settlers to fight off the Danish ships. The settlers refused to violate their oath of loyalty to Denmark, in spite of Milan's threats of imprisonment. They were then persuaded by Milan's threat of the gallows, a threat that could not be ignored on the basis of less than a year of Milan's administration, to sign a statement that they would rather leave St Thomas than be separated from their governor. Milan sought to hire mercenaries in the French islands and sent a ship to raid Puerto Rico to acquire funds for what he considered his private war with the West India Company.

There was, however, no resistance when Commissioner Mikkel Mikkelsen arrived aboard the *Fortuna*. Hearings were held, but there was 'so much shrieking, shouting, and screaming' that the secretary was unable to keep his records straight. The clearly deranged Governor Milan and former Governor Adolph Esmit were returned to Denmark to stand trial, along with Nicolai Esmit, who had been imprisoned by his brother and sent back to Copenhagen, where he was still incarcerated.

Christopher Heins became Acting Governor and instituted the first in a series of sound administrations which resulted in the steady growth of the Danish colony. The West India Company, however, was in serious difficulty. In order to secure capital after six years of mismanagement and losses, the directors involved the Company in two nearly desperate schemes.

The Duke of Brandenburg, whose heirs were to become the kings of Prussia, had financed the Brandenburger Company for slave trade with

Contemporary portrait of King Christian V and Queen Charlotte Amalie of Denmark, 1697.

5

the Americas. This company had stations, called barracoons, on the Gold Coast of Africa, where slaves were purchased and held for shipment, but it needed a base in the West Indies, where the human cargo could be marketed. In 1685 a treaty was signed with Denmark, allowing the Brandenburger Company to trade and to establish a 'factory' on St Thomas, in return for paying land rents and duties on imports and exports. It was also stipulated that a plantation had to be cultivated and taxes on its produce paid to the West India Company. The Germans were not to deal with freebooters or trade in condemned prizes. This treaty was to remain in effect for 30 years, but it included provisions for renegotiating terms.

In 1687, less than a year after the Brandenburger Company had established its St Thomas base, serious friction developed with the West India Company. The Germans fell behind on their payments, did not cultivate their plantation, and competed with the West India Company for trade.

In 1690 the Brandenburger Company directors, in an effort to cut expenses, leased St Thomas with its administration for a period of 10 years to the Norweigan merchant George Thormuellen. In return for a full use of the Company's island properties and a monopoly on the West Indian trade, Thormoellen was to pay an anuual rent based on 4 per cent of the Company's investment and, at his own expense, maintain a garrison, a governor and all other functionaries of the establishment. This second scheme added further complications to the already difficult situations existing on St Thomas. It brought losses, both for the lessee and the Company's stockholders. The lease was terminated in 1694, but suits in court delayed a final settlement for several years.

From then on the Brandenburger Company relied only on its own trained people for the administration of the colony and, in the early eighteenth century, entered its first period of prosperity.

The cause of St Thomas's accelerated growth in the early eighteenth century was the war of the Spanish succession (1701–13) which involved all of the European nations with colonies in the Caribbean except Denmark, making Charlotte Amalie the only neutral harbor in the region. Dutch, English, and French traders flocked to the island to pursue the transit trade among the warring parties and other nations. There were 160 plantations under cultivation on St Thomas and the West India Company showed profits for two decades.

Peace brought a reduction of trade. The produce, (sugar, cotton, indigo, and the like) from other islands no longer came through St Thomas on its way to Europe and the plantations on St Thomas did not produce enough to maintain the West India Company's profits.

Governor Iversen had, in 1675, claimed unsettled St John, as the Company's charter empowered him to do. In earlier years parties from St Thomas had visited this island for logging and some had remained long enough to plant and harvest a crop before they were chased off by the English from Tortola. In 1717 planters, supported by a small garrison, took formal possession of St John. Similar attempts had been made to claim Vieques, but its proximity to Puerto Rico and frequent visits by Spanish forces had discouraged settlement.

The British reacted quickly. Governor General Hamilton of the Leeward Islands sent a man-of-war to Charlotte Amalie to deliver the ultimatum that unless the Danes withdrew from St John, forceful seizure of both St Thomas and St John might ensue. Governor Bredal, supported by the West India Company, refused to comply. The case was referred to the home governments, which took until 1762 to reach a diplomatic settlement. The Court of St James finally decided that a diplomatic rupture with Denmark-Norway was not worth a small, dry, and rocky Caribbean island. Thus St John became part of the Danish West Indies. Practically all of St John had been parcelled out in plantations by 1722, and cultivation was encouraged through five-year tax easements.

This considerable increase in the colony's arable land was still inadequate to meet the demand for sugar and other tropical products. In the late 1720s overtures were made to Louis XV of France for the purchase of St Croix. This island had been a no-man's-land since 1695, when its colonists had been pressed to move to St Dominique, present-day Haiti, to bolster this larger and more important French colony. A treaty was finalized in 1733 and Denmark took possession in September 1734. St Croix with its plains and gently rolling hills is far better suited to cultivation than St Thomas and St John, 40 miles to the north; it is also larger than the latter two islands combined. Its development proceeded rapidly, partly at the expense of St Thomas and St John, many of whose settlers acquired plantations and moved to St Croix. These settlers were attracted by the higher returns promised by St Croix and were discouraged by recent events on St John.

In late 1733 the slaves of St John revolted; they controlled the island for nearly six months. Early on the morning of Monday 23 November, about a dozen of the Company's slaves came to the small fort overlooking Coral Bay carrying bundles of firewood. The sentry allowed them to enter and was immediately cut down by the blacks who had hidden cane knives in their bundles. The sleeping garrison was then killed, except for one soldier who managed to hide. The slaves fired three cannon shots to signal that the fort was taken and a general uprising followed. Bands of blacks roamed the plantations, killing any whites they found. Cornelius Bodger was spared because the blacks needed his medical skills; his two young sons, because they were needed as servants; and a former overseer, because of his acts of mercy towards slaves while he served the Company.

Many planters escaped, some warned by their own slaves. The surviving planters with their faithful Negroes gathered at Peter Durloo's plantation on the north-east point of St John, where they prepared themselves for the rebels' attack. It came later in the afternoon and continued intermittently through the night and into the next day. On 24 November, fewer than 20 reinforcements arrived from St Thomas, which enabled the defenders to persist.

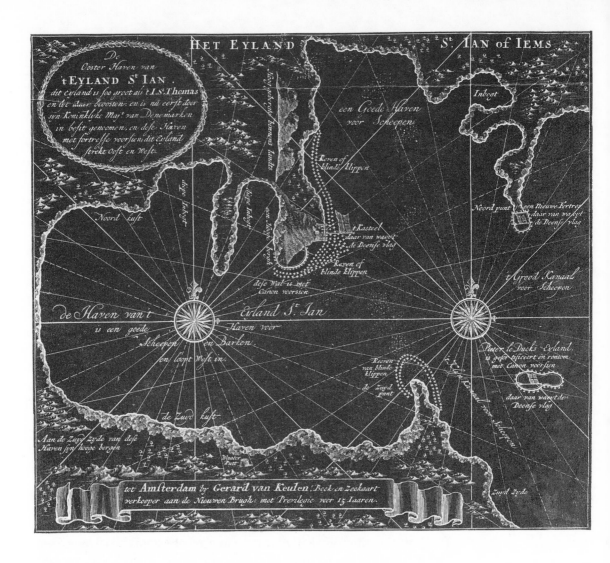

*Map of Coral Bay,
St John, 1719.*

Attack and counterattack continued for six months. The fort at Coral Bay was recaptured and then abandoned. The rebels were scattered over the island and elusive. Attempts to capture them with English assistance failed. An appeal for help was made to the French in Martinique, who sent two boats with 220 Creole troops and officers. The Danes contributed about 100 militiamen, both black and white, and a grim chase, lasting about a month, followed. Some rebels were killed, others gave themselves up, and several, realizing the hopelessness of their situation, committed suicide. In fact, 11 bodies were found near Ram's Head and another 25 at Brown Bay on the northeast coast — the remains of two mass suicides. Although 15 managed to hide in the bush for a few months, they were captured and brought to trial. About a dozen rebels were tortured, and executed by burning, dismemberment, or impalement.

Of the 92 plantations on St John at the time of the rebellion, 48 suffered damage. About a quarter of both the black and white populations lost their lives. Recovery was slow, partly due to an exodus to St Croix, and in 1735 only 62 plantations had resumed cultivation. St John did recuperate and in 1780 reached its peak development as a plantation society. But the memory of the holocaust poisoned the relationship between the races on St John for many decades.

Two main causes of the St John revolt are easily identified. Many of the slaves involved were recently arrived from Africa, rather than more docile Creoles born in the West Indies, and conditions on the plantations were unusually severe, with some slaves actually dying of starvation. The African slaves were often proud, and many had been nobles and slave-owners themselves. There are documented cases of such persons starving themselves to death rather than working as slaves. Conditions for slaves on St John were appalling by today's standards. In 1733 a drought, destructive hurricane, and plague of insects had depleted crops. Slaves produced their own food to a large extent and were threatened with famine. The whites on the island, outnumbered five to one in a population of 1300, felt threatened and pressed the government for a new, harsher slave code, which was published in September 1733. It was of such severity that it can only be understood as an attempt to terrorize the starving Negro population. The whites clearly underestimated the martial skills of some of their slaves, some of whom had apparently commanded African armies. The Africans seem to have correctly gauged the local opposition, and they probably could have held St John indefinitely if no outside military force had been available. This is being written during the 250th anniversary of the event and we recommend both historical and fictional accounts, listed at the end of this work.

The West India Company was by its charter both a plantation and a trading company. The colony was both its supplier and its market and, in the three islands, the Company was both landlord and government. It set the rules and the prices, and it monopolized all legal trade. The privy council, which comprised the governor and his chief officers, was the final authority as well as the high court of the islands. There was a common council of burghers and planters that acted as both lower court and advisory board to the governor, but had no legislative or executive powers. With the colony's rapid growth in the early eighteenth century, there emerged a prosperous class of merchants and planters who objected to the Company's broad monopolies. In 1706 and 1715 this group sent delegations to Copenhagen to present their case to the Danish Government. They achieved some easement of taxes and trade restrictions, but their petition for representative government was denied. Such concessions did not pacify the planters and merchants, whose influence continued to increase along with their wealth and numbers. In 1746 they proposed that the Danish Government take over the administration of the islands. A similar proposal was submitted in 1754 and was approved by the Danish State Board of Trade. The following year, King Frederik V acted on this proposal, buying out all the shares of the West India Company. By this simple transaction St Thomas, St John, and St Croix became crown colonies. Trade between Denmark-Norway and its overseas possessions, which previously had been the West India Company's exclusive privilege, was now opened to all its subjects.

During the 1740s and 1750s St Croix developed rapidly, its population increasing to 10,330 — nearly double that of St Thomas and St John combined. The colony's capital was moved from Charlotte Amalie to Christiansted, now the larger town. St Croix was productive beyond expectation and developed a typical plantation economy. While agriculture continued on St Thomas, trade became its main source of wealth.

The late eighteenth century was a period of great wealth in the Danish West Indies. Charlotte Amalie grew and by the century's end was once again larger than Christiansted. Denmark-Norway remained neutral in the European wars of this period and the West Indian transit trade had to pass through St Thomas's harbor as it had at the beginning of the eighteenth century. New free trade laws, allowing ships of all nations to load and unload at Charlotte Amalie, made St Thomas the most important harbor in the West Indies. The 1792 law prohibiting citizens of Denmark-Norway to trade in slaves did not adversely affect this.

With the Napoleonic Wars, conditions changed abruptly. Relations between Britain and Denmark-Norway were strained during the last years of the eighteenth century, because some Danish merchant ships had been seized as prizes of war. The British were blockading France and they demanded that Denmark-Norway not trade with France or her allies. As a countermeasure, Denmark-Norway entered into a 'neutrality pact' with Sweden and Russia, and began to convoy its merchantmen. Britain considered Denmark-Norway an ally of France and in April 1801 the English fleet, under Parker and Nelson, bombarded Copenhagen.

Three weeks before the shelling of Copenhagen, a large British force occupied the Danish West Indies — St Croix, St John, and St Thomas. There was no resistance to the invasion and the colonial government managed to negotiate an accommodation with the occupying forces. It

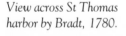
View across St Thomas harbor by Bradt, 1780.

was agreed that the islands were taken peacefully and not in an act of war. This allowed the civilian administration to continue, rather than be replaced by the military. British army and navy units remained on all three islands, with a fortified base on the St Thomas peninsula which is now Hassel Island. After less than a year, the islands were returned to Denmark in February 1802.

During the early nineteenth century, Denmark-Norway had the largest navy and merchant fleet in Europe after Britain. Controlled by France, this force could pose a serious threat. By 1807 the British apparently decided that use of the fleets of Denmark-Norway would be one of the few remaining means by which Napoleon could 'snatch victory from the jaws of defeat', so they again sent their navy into Charlotte Amalie. Simultaneously, an English envoy sought out the Danish regent, Crown Prince Frederik, to demand that Denmark-Norway enter into an alliance with England and that the entire navy of Denmark-Norway be handed over to Britain for the duration of the war with Napoleon. The regent refused and the British invaded Copenhagen, causing many fatalities and serious damage by naval bombardment, and capturing much of the Danish fleet and naval stores. War was declared on Britain, which ultimately resulted in the dissolution of the 400-year union between Norway and Denmark.

The British occupied the Danish islands from 1807 to 1815, when they were once more returned to Denmark. The first occupation, in 1801–2, had been brief and had not seriously affected the islands' economy. The second British occupation left deeper scars. St Thomas's trade stagnated and the planters, blocked from their markets, were impoverished. Denmark had fallen on hard times during the war years; her fleet was lost, her capital was bombarded and raided, and she was divorced from Norway — no financial assistance for the West Indian colony was forthcoming from that quarter. The sugar economy of the islands was now feeling the competition of other areas in the New World better suited to modern methods of cane cultivation and was soon to suffer even more from the cultivation of sugar beets in Europe. Although St Croix still appeared relatively prosperous, its economy was starting to falter by the 1830s. In 1848 slavery was abolished in the Danish West Indies. For St Croix, this was just another step in the long, slow decline of its plantation economy, which started with the Napoleonic Wars and extended to the final abandonment of sugar cane cultivation in the mid-1960s.

On the mountainous terrain of St John, agricultural pursuits had already slowed by the end of the eighteenth century, and by the late nineteenth century they had collapsed. Plantations changed hands with increasing rapidity to settle debts and were then abandoned. Attempts to keep the old ways going by turning to animal husbandry, fruit, and ground provisions (yams, tanias etc.) failed. One plantation on St John, the Reef Bay Estate, raised sugar cane until the 1920s, but this was for local consumption and out of the pride of the owner.

After 1815, St Thomas fared better than its sister islands. It was not deeply affected by the decline of the sugar economy, as its harbor had already replaced agriculture as the main source of revenue. To help its recovery from the British occupation, St Thomas and St John were made free ports in 1815. By 1820, St Thomas was once again a shipping center and major distribution point. For the next half century it was a flourishing commercial port and a large part of all West Indian trade was channelled through its harbor. It owed this dominant position in Caribbean commercial life to the excellence of its harbor and ship repair facilities, a well organized banking system, adequate capital, favorable credit terms, and an aggressive merchant group. In 1845 Charlotte Amalie had 41 large importing houses and 60 smaller ones. These businesses were owned by Englishmen, Frenchmen, Germans, Haitians, Spaniards, Americans, Sephardim, and Danes; the population was as cosmopolitan as any in the world.

Steamships began to replace sailing vessels in the 1840s and St Thomas became the coaling and watering station for ships running between South America and North Atlantic ports. Shipping lines made Charlotte Amalie their headquarters and St Thomas became a communication, as well as distribution, center.

The technological advancement of steamships and the political climate made it possible for Spanish and English Caribbean islands to import directly from producers, and by the 1860s it was apparent that Charlotte Amalie's half century of prosperity was coming to an end. Cholera and malaria epidemics in the 1850s had tarnished St Thomas's reputation as a healthy island. Its reputation as a safe harbor was also lost when in October 1867 the island was hit by a violent hurricane that did tremendous damage. In November, several severe earthquakes and a 27-foot tidal wave (tsunami) devastated the harbor. Several naive people

St Thomas harbor after the tsunami of 18 November 1867, reproduced from an engraving which appeared in The Times *of London.*

were killed by the tidal wave because they walked out into the harbor floor as it drained. Other more knowledgeable citizens headed for high ground and escaped the wall of water which swept all before it. St Thomas's trade declined rapidly, but it remained an important coaling port into the early twentieth century, when this source of revenue also dried up as ships switched to oil fuel.

The prosperity of St Thomas during the early and mid-nineteenth century was not sufficient to counter the failing plantation economies of St John and St Croix, and the Danish West Indies became more and more dependent on the Danish treasury. During the Civil War in the United States, the Union had great difficulty blockading the Confederacy due to the proximity of many West Indian ports. After the war, the United States recognized that it had strategic interests in the Caribbean which could be served by the establishment of naval bases there. In 1865 the first overtures were made in Copenhagen for the purchase of the Danish West Indies. Denmark was receptive, not only because the islands had become an economic liability, but also because recent military defeats had caused the home economy to decline. A plebiscite held in the islands was almost unanimously in favor of the transfer and a treaty was drawn up between the two governments. The United States Senate, however, refused to ratify the treaty, and it was allowed to lapse.

New negotiations were initiated in 1901 and a treaty was formulated, but this time the Danish Senate failed to confirm it. In 1911–12 the scheme was considered again, but did not reach treaty stage. During the First World War the United States again approached Denmark for the purchase of the islands, and this time succeeded. Voters both in the islands and in Denmark voted to approve the sale. On 17 January 1917 sovereignty passed to the United States, Denmark having been paid $25 million, and the territory became the United States (US) Virgin Islands.

The US Navy administered the now renamed Virgin Islands until 1931. During this time, major social reforms were accomplished, some public works projects were completed, and Prohibition played havoc with what international shipping was still using Charlotte Amalie harbor. Ships coming into the harbor had all alcohol on board confiscated, even if it was not to be unloaded. They therefore went elsewhere until Prohibition was repealed. The adoption of the name 'Virgin Islands' for the former Danish West Indies is curious in itself. It is not entirely clear which part of the archipelago Columbus had named in honor of the 11,000 martyred virgins — he may well have been to the east of St John at the time — but he certainly did not include St Croix. In any case, the British colony had had exclusive use of the name for three centuries until it was usurped by the United States, forcing it to add 'British' to its name. This was not the first time the United States had stolen a name; millions of other inhabitants of the Western Hemisphere have a right to use 'American' and it is not coincidence that Spanish has the word 'estado-unidense' meaning citizen of the United States.

In 1936 Congress passed the first Organic Act of the Virgin Islands

Modern Charlotte Amalie, St Thomas. Fort Christian (right) and the Legislature Building (left) are clearly visible in the foreground. Veterans' Drive runs between these two buildings and along the harbor edge. Behind it, in the centre of the picture, numerous old warehouses can be seen running back along narrow alleys at right angles to the waterfront.

which, in effect, was their first constitution, bringing some self-government to the Territory. Amendments to the Organic Act have since passed many additional facets of government to local control, while others still, in 1985, remain under federal control, most notably the courts of law.

Tourism became a significant source of income in the 1950s. After 1959, when Cuba was closed to Americans, it expanded very rapidly. In the 1960s, industries, such as petroleum and bauxite refining and watch assembly, were established and sugar production finally disappeared from the Virgin Islands.

Today, St Thomas continues its history as the most cosmopolitan of the islands, St Croix remains the most rural, and St John is still a sparsely inhabited satellite. The imprint of history can be discerned in the dialects, cultures, cuisines, and architectures of the three islands, which are decidedly distinct. In the following chapters we will explore the architecture of St Thomas and St John, fitting it into the historic context outlined here.

2 The Commercial District

Charlotte Amalie was neither planned nor planned for by the Danish West India Company. During its first decades of settlement, St Thomas developed as a plantation society, but, even before the Danish acquisition of St John, perceptive traders and planters realized that the commercial harbor offered potentially greater profits than the agricultural pursuits of the island's plantations. The growth of Charlotte Amalie was accordingly dictated by the economics and other demands of trade. It was founded in 1681 when four artisans were allowed to build their homes west of Fort Christian, beyond the area reserved for the West India Company's buildings, and were granted licenses as innkeepers. Named Charlotte Amalie from the start, in honor of the Danish Queen, the village was popularly known as 'Taphuus', meaning pub. It was a name that was used well into the eighteenth century and stemmed from its modest beginnings. The town grew slowly as a single row of houses on the north, landward side of the seaside road, now Main Street (Dronningens Gade in Danish), running from the fort to the west end of the island.

Père Jean Batiste Labat, a French Dominican missionary who travelled widely in the Caribbean in the early 1700s, recorded his detailed impressions of his two visits to St Thomas. He described Charlotte Amalie in 1700 as a proper little town of one street of buildings in the Dutch style, with whitewashed interiors. Père Labat reestablished his friendship with a French lady whom he had known in Martinique, and made several bargain purchases on St Thomas, including some yardage of oriental muslin, which he claimed was less expensive here than elsewhere in the West Indies or in Europe. He enjoyed St Thomas's freewheeling atmosphere, while other, more puritanical observers called it a den of pirates at this time. Père Labat found the Governor and the head of the Brandenburger Company knowledgeable and well informed.

The basic pattern of Chrlotte Amalie's development was established during its first decades. The village was sited on well drained land close to the modern port, between the two stream beds or guts that run down through the valleys flanking Denmark Hill. The beach fronting the

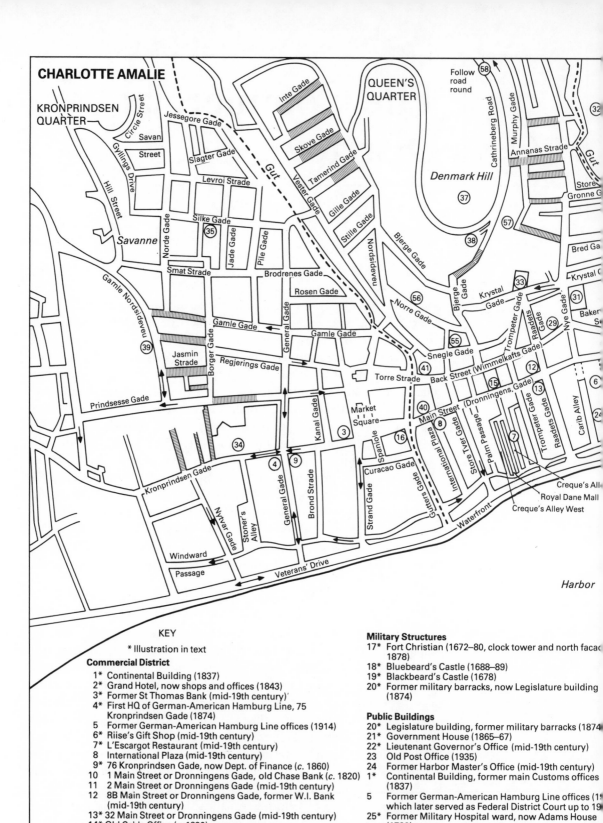

CHARLOTTE AMALIE

KRONPRINDSEN QUARTER

QUEEN'S QUARTER

Follow road round

Circle Street

Savan Street

Gyllings Drive

Hill Street

Savanne

Jessegore Gade

Slagter Gade

Levroi Strade

Silke Gade

Norde Gade

Jade Gade

Pile Gade

Smat Strade

Gamle Nordsideveu

Jasmin Strade

Borger Gade

Gamle Gade

Regjerings Gade

Prindsesse Gade

Inte Gade

Skove Gade

Tamerind Gade

Gille Gade

Stille Gade

Vester Gade

Gut

Brodrenes Gade

Rosen Gade

Gamle Gade

General Gade

Nordsideveu

Denmark Hill

Bjerge Gade

Norre Gade

Snegle Gade

Bjerge Gade

Krystal Gade

Trompeter Gade

Wimmelkafts Gade

Back Street

Torre Strade

Market Square

Spaniole

Kanal Gade

Curacao Gade

Kronprindsen Gade

General Gade

Brond Strade

Strand Gade

Nyvar Gade

Stoner's Alley

Windward Passage

Veterans' Drive

Gutters Gade

International Plaza

Main Street (Dronningens Gade)

Store Tver Gade

Palm Passage

Dronningens Gade

Trompeter Gade

Raadets Gade

Carib Alley

Waterfront

Creque's Alley
Royal Dane Mall
Creque's Alley West

Harbor

Cathrineberg Road

Murphy Gade

Annanas Strade

Gronne G

Bred Ga

Krystal C

Baker S

Nye Gade

Raadets

Store

Gut

KEY

* Illustration in text

Commercial District

1* Continental Building (1837)
2* Grand Hotel, now shops and offices (1843)
3* Former St Thomas Bank (mid-19th century)
4* First HQ of German-American Hamburg Line, 75 Kronprindsen Gade (1874)
5 Former German-American Hamburg Line offices (1914)
6* Riise's Gift Shop (mid-19th century)
7* L'Escargot Restaurant (mid-19th century)
8 International Plaza (mid-19th century)
9* 76 Kronprindsen Gade, now Dept. of Finance (c. 1860)
10 1 Main Street or Dronningens Gade, old Chase Bank (c. 1820)
11 2 Main Street or Dronningens Gade (mid-19th century)
12 8B Main Street or Dronningens Gade, former W.I. Bank (mid-19th century)
13* 32 Main Street or Dronningens Gade (mid-19th century)
14* Old Cable Office (c. 1890)
15 Camile Pissaro Building (mid-19th century)
16* 84 Kronprindsen Gade, warehouse (mid-19th century)

Military Structures

17* Fort Christian (1672–80, clock tower and north facad 1878)
18* Bluebeard's Castle (1688–89)
19* Blackbeard's Castle (1678)
20* Former military barracks, now Legislature building (1874)

Public Buildings

20* Legislature building, former military barracks (1874
21* Government House (1865–67)
22* Lieutenant Governor's Office (mid-19th century)
23 Old Post Office (1935)
24 Former Harbor Master's Office (mid-19th century)
1* Continental Building, former main Customs offices (1837)
5 Former German-American Hamburg Line offices (1 which later served as Federal District Court up to 19
25* Former Military Hospital ward, now Adams House (1799)
26* Old Hospital (late 19th century)
27 Department of Education, 43 Kongens Gade (c. 187

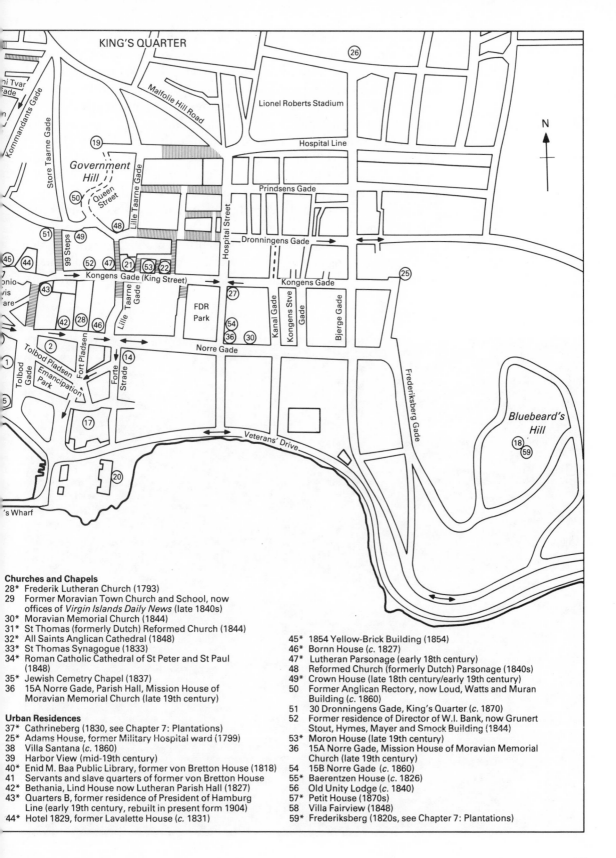

Churches and Chapels

28* Frederik Lutheran Church (1793)
29 Former Moravian Town Church and School, now
     offices of *Virgin Islands Daily News* (late 1840s)
30* Moravian Memorial Church (1844)
31* St Thomas (formerly Dutch) Reformed Church (1844)
32* All Saints Anglican Cathedral (1848)
33* St Thomas Synagogue (1833)
34* Roman Catholic Cathedral of St Peter and St Paul
     (1848)
35* Jewish Cemetry Chapel (1837)
36 15A Norre Gade, Parish Hall, Mission House of
     Moravian Memorial Church (late 19th century)

Urban Residences

37* Cathrineberg (1830, see Chapter 7: Plantations)
25* Adams House, former Military Hospital ward (1799)
38* Villa Santana (*c.* 1860)
39 Harbor View (mid-19th century)
40* Enid M. Baa Public Library, former von Bretton House (1818)
41 Servants and slave quarters of former von Bretton House
42* Bethania, Lind House now Lutheran Parish Hall (1827)
43* Quarters B, former residence of President of Hamburg
     Line (early 19th century, rebuilt in present form 1904)
44* Hotel 1829, former Lavalette House (*c.* 1831)

45* 1854 Yellow-Brick Building (1854)
46* Born House (*c.* 1827)
47* Lutheran Parsonage (early 18th century)
48 Reformed Church (formerly Dutch) Parsonage (1840s)
49* Crown House (late 18th century/early 19th century)
50 Former Anglican Rectory, now Loud, Watts and Muran
     Building (*c.* 1860)
51 30 Dronningens Gade, King's Quarter (*c.* 1870)
52 Former residence of Director of W.I. Bank, now Grunert
     Stout, Hymes, Mayer and Smock Building (1844)
53* Moron House (late 19th century)
36 15A Norre Gade, Mission House of Moravian Memorial
     Church (late 19th century)
54 15B Norre Gade (*c.* 1860)
55* Baerentzen House (*c.* 1826)
56 Old Unity Lodge (*c.* 1840)
57* Petit House (1870s)
58 Villa Fairview (1848)
59* Frederiksberg (1820s, see Chapter 7: Plantations)

village allowed ships to come relatively close to the shore. The planters who enforced trade and who, in 1692, were granted lots for warehouses built them on the seaward side of the road. Although the seventeenth and eighteenth century buildings are no more, there are still warehouses on the south side of Main Street and residences and shops along the north side. The guts that a few decades ago were covered over are still the boundaries between Kronprindsen Quarter to the west, Queen's Quarter in the centre and King's Quarter to the east. East of the port the shoreline was backed by a lagoon. It was filled in during the late-eighteenth century but King's Quarter never developed the same pattern of building types along the shoreline as in Queen's Quarter and Kronprindsen Quarter.

As trade accelerated in the eighteenth century, the strip of land suitable for loading and unloading vessels became extremely valuable. It increased in cost and in significance to Charlotte Amalie's merchants,

Chart of St Thomas harbor by Gerard van Keulen, 1719.

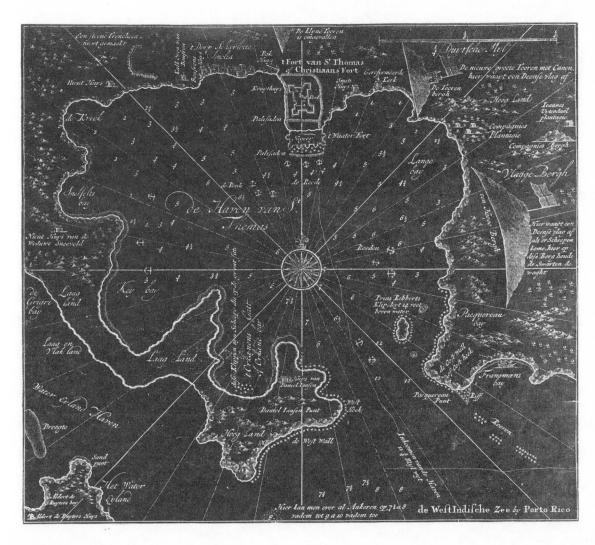

The landing place, known as King's Wharf, at Charlotte Amalie, 1930.

whose access to the harbor was of paramount importance to the success of their trade. As a result, the shoreline was subdivided into the very deep and narrow lots which are still characteristic of this part of town. The demand for loading facilities and warehouse space caused extension of the same type of development westward, so that, by the first decade of the nineteenth century, several additional city blocks along the shoreline had been subdivided into narrow lots. To provide more space and greater water depths, most of these lots were extended into the water by landfill. The rows of warehouses faced the harbor. Each had its pier or slip and, in many of the narrow alleys — streets would have claimed too much valuable real estate — there were hand carts on rails for distributing goods to the warehouses and stores which now flanked both sides of the main street.

By the 1940s, automobile traffic was seriously congesting the streets of Charlotte Amalie; to alleviate it, the present waterfront highway, Veterans' Drive, was constructed on landfill in front of the commercial properties. It was completed in the early 1950s, landlocking the warehouse area and eliminating the small boat basin at King's Wharf just west of Fort Christian.

On the landside of Main Street, the village spread up the lower slopes of Denmark and Government Hills that surrounded the older section of Charlotte Amalie, and then it spread up the valley between them. It was an uncontrolled growth and the irregularities of the terrain resulted in odd-shaped blocks separated by narrow lanes and general congestion.

Charlotte Amalie was a fully-fledged town by the mid-1700s and was so crowded that the government had to identify new residential areas, especially for the free colored, as the manumitted slaves were called. The free coloreds already comprised a substantial segment of the population and formed a middle class of artisans, clerks, and shopkeepers. In 1764–5, the valley west of Denmark Hill, named Savanne, was surveyed and subdivided for their use. During the same years, the valley east of Government Hill was divided into lots for the white population of the town. Both areas were laid out in a regular grid pattern, in contrast with the irregular arrangement at the center of town.

By the early 1800s Charlotte Amalie extended along the shoreline to both the east and west and up the sides of Government, Denmark, Frenchman, and Bluebeard's Hills. The hillsides, though steep and difficult construction sites, became the preferred residential areas for the views of town and harbor they afforded and for their cooling trade wind breezes.

Charlotte Amalie has been a disaster-prone town. It has been hit repeatedly by destructive hurricanes and earthquakes and has been ravaged by fires, which have caused the greatest damage. Between 1804 and 1832, six fires destroyed two-thirds of the town. The enormity of these fires was the result of uncontrolled growth in the eighteenth

Masonry details of the warehouse building on the corner of Gutters Gade and Market Square, Charlotte Amalie.

century, when mostly-wood structures were built close together on streets which were no more than narrow lanes. After the three fires in 1804 and 1806, some old streets were widened, new streets built, and the construction of masonry warehouses encouraged. These measures were inadequate and two more major fires devastated the western and central quarters of Charlotte Amalie in 1825 and 1826. Soon thereafter, the town's first building code was enacted, but the fires continued. A disastrous fire broke out on Old Year's Eve 1831 (called New Year's Eve elsewhere), which continued through New Year's Day. A far more restrictive building code was enacted that same month, January 1832. It prohibited wood buildings on Main Street between its east end and the Catholic Church and required, among other things, that all new roofs were to be covered with fire-resistant materials. Wood shingles, previously the most common roofing material, had to be replaced with tile or slate when repairs were effected. To encourage rebuilding, the government offered tax-free loans for masonry construction.

While many fire-resistant warehouses and masonry shops and residences had already been built by 1831, favorable financing, reduced insurance rates, and increased property values caused their number to increase during the following decades. In the warehouse district south of Main Street, the so-called 'Fireproof' proliferated. This characteristic building type is hardly fireproof, but its sturdy construction of heavy masonry walls and roofs of several layers of brick over a web of small and large beams has remained serviceable up to the present. Metal or metal-covered shutters, as well as double-planked wooden ones, still protect the interiors. In a few cases the builders resorted to pure masonry construction with vaulted interiors or, when funds or materials were not available, more conventional roof forms of wood trusses covered with sheet metal. Strictly utilitarian in purpose, these warehouses impress mainly by their straightforward construction and their simplicity. Their

Riise's Gift Shop in Charlotte Amalie which still exhibits the solid construction of its original warehouse use.

arched masonry partitions leave a spacious interior appropriate for the tropics.

The material generally used in older masonry construction in the Virgin Islands was a rubble mix of field stone and brick bats set in mortar. Brick was used in the framing of window and door openings, arches and cornices. Both interior and exterior walls were then given protective coats of plaster. The finer details — cornices, banding, and other ornamentation — were added in the final coats of plaster. Such ornamentation was concentrated on the Main Street and seaward fronts of the warehouses, which exhibit a great variety of treatments. In a few cases, larger budgets and ambitions resulted in brick or cut stone construction which was not covered with plaster. In recent years, many rubble walls have been stripped of their plaster, exposing interesting patterns of brick and blue bitch stone (a volcanic tuff). Unfortunately, such stripped walls deteriorate fairly rapidly, especially when exposed to weather.

On the north side of Main Street and Kronprindsen Gade beyond, the emphasis was on shops, rather than warehouses, and the ground floors contained large open spaces adaptable to a variety of uses. Second floor residences were the norm on this side of the street, while they were the exception over the warehouses. Only a few of these buildings have interior stairways, the more typical arrangement being an exterior masonry staircase, often of impressive proportions, in a courtyard at the rear of the building. These courtyards served as an extension of the residential space above, containing cisterns, kitchens, and, in the case

Wrought and cast-iron balconies on Kronprindsen Gade west of the Roman Catholic Cathedral, Charlotte Amalie. Also see the pictures on pages 24 and 25.

of the largest establishments, slave quarters and stables. In their use of materials, construction, and ornamentation, these buildings are similar to those of the warehouses across the street.

The architectural treatment of the commercial district does not conform to any of the standard stylistic categories such as baroque, classical revival, or regency. The creators of these buildings, inhabitants of a cosmopolitan port, were exposed to many influences. They were also constrained by climate, site, and the desired functions of the structures. Additional formative factors were the availability of materials, as well as local construction techniques and skills. These influences and conditions combined to produce an architecture of adaptation with a strong character unique to the Danish West Indies. Even the occasional 'high style' buildings, including many churches, which can be assigned to one or another European stylistic category, exhibit features which make them uniquely island creations.

The ornamentation on buildings in the commercial district is very restrained. Banding of window and door openings is common. Most buildings have simplified classical cornices and banding or pilasters at the corners. Many of the two-story structures have balconies over the street, some with elaborate cast-iron railings and supporting brackets, while others show simpler wrought-iron or wood detailing.

St Thomas harbor, although no longer the transit market and shipping center it was in the days of sail and early steamboats, is still a busy port. Cruise ships visit almost every day, and there are often several in the harbor at once. The trader has been replaced by the tourist. He comes by airplane or for a brief visit on one of the cruise lines to appreciate the beauty of St Thomas and to enjoy the various facilities offered by Charlotte Amalie. The town is still business oriented, and Main Street from the Grand Hotel to Market Square — the old commercial district — is now an open-air shopping mall which branches off into alleys and streets leading down to the water front, between the old warehouses. The former St Thomas Bank on Market Square is worthy of note. There have been many changes to this historic district in the last few decades, but it has preserved much of its original character and appearance. Main Street itself is flanked by one-, two-, and three-story buildings which form a harmonious streetscape in spite of their various heights. The ground floors of these buildings still serve as shops, as they did originally, while the upper floors, once residences, are now mostly offices.

The astute observer will find many buildings to admire along and just off Main Street. We will discuss some typical examples and point out a few with special qualities. In the latter category is the two-story, reinforced concrete structure located directly west of Fort Christian and facing Emancipation Park. It once served as the District Court and now contains government offices, including the Office of Tourism. Designed by the German architect J. P. Schmit and completed in 1914, it originally had a small, truncated tower over its southeast corner, which,

Market Square and former St Thomas Bank, Charlotte Amalie.

*Detail of former
St Thomas Bank,
5 Kronprindsen Gade,
Charlotte Amalie.*

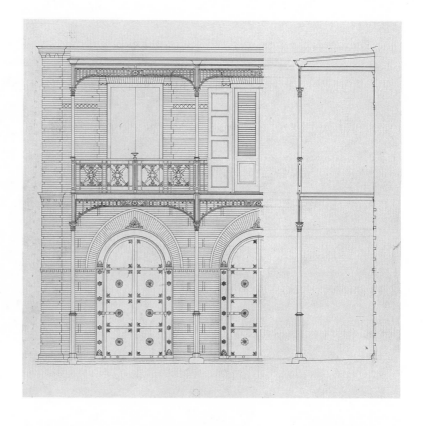

*Below:
View looking west down
Main Street, Charlotte
Amalie, 1880. Notice
the warehouse gates on
the left and the shops with
second floor residences on
the right.*

First headquarters of the German-American Hamburg Line at 75 Kronprindsen Gade, Charlotte Amalie.

Continental Building, Charlotte Amalie.

for unknown reasons, was torn down. Originally the offices of the German-American Hamburg Line, which made St Thomas its West Indian headquarters for half a century, this building is an important early example of the International Style. It was a forerunner to the simple lines and starkness of the Bauhaus school, which influenced most contemporary architecture.

Immediately to the north is the Continental Building and, facing onto the north side of Emancipation Park, the Grand Hotel. Both are typical examples of Charlotte Amalie's architectural traditions. The Continental Building, with its striated yellow brick facade, ground floor arcade, and symmetrical fenestrations has an eighteenth century feel, but was built after 1837. The Grand Hotel, more timely in design, was inaugurated in 1843 and served as a hotel until 1975. It now houses shops on

Grand Hotel, Charlotte Amalie.

Interior of L'Escargot restaurant, an adaptive use of an old warehouse on Main Street, Charlotte Amalie.

Creque's Alley, one of the numerous alleys leading from Main Street down to the water front, Charlotte Amalie.

the ground floor, offices in the former guest rooms, and a restaurant in the large, open lobby on the second floor.

Some impression of what the interiors of St Thomas warehouses were like in the mid-nineteenth century can be had by visiting Riise's Gift Shop, Riise's Liquors, and L'Escargot Restaurant. All three still show the original construction with beamed ceilings and boldly arched partitions. L'Escargot is located in one of the three Creque's Alleys — formerly a single warehouse complex, which now houses gift shops. Creque's Alleys provide a good idea of the extensive storage facilities required by a trading concern in Charlotte Amalie's heyday.

A common plan was the double warehouse, with a courtyard separating symmetrical buildings. These courtyards were designed as private work areas, not the public walkways they have become. Palm Passage is one such courtyard. Another example has been preserved in International Plaza. Its one-story facade on Main Street (22 Dronningens Gade) has three bays, expressing the two rows of warehouses flanking a center courtyard extending to the water's edge. Pilasters flank the gateway and accentuate the corners of the building. They support a finely carved

Above:
Palm Passage, a greatly altered courtyard off Main Street which was once the commercial headquarters of A. Vance & Co., Charlotte Amalie.

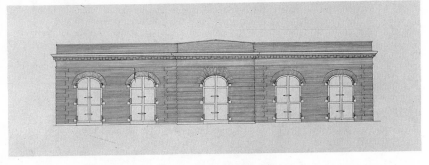

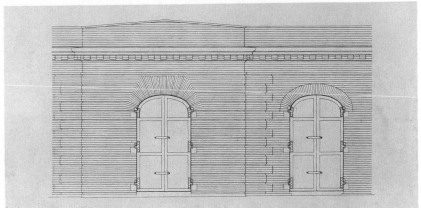

Drawing of 76 Kronprindsen Gade, Charlotte Amalie (front elevation and detail).

76 Kronprindsen Gade,
Charlotte Amalie.

32 Dronningens Gade,
Charlotte Amalie.

sandstone cornice crowned by a panelled parapet wall. Although the courtyard and the warehouses survive, they have been marred by the recent addition of a second story.

Further west on Main Street, at 76 Kronprindsen Gade, is another example of double warehouse layout. The courtyard here has been

Old Cable Office, on the corner of Norre Gade and Forte Street, Charlotte Amalie.

obliterated by modern construction, but the surviving Main Street facade, finished in brick, is distinctive. The center bay, with its archway to the previous courtyard, is projected and highly rusticated. It is flanked by two bays with less baroque treatments and crowned by a brick cornice with an exaggerated dentil course and a banded parapet wall. The five doorways on Main Street have retained their heavy metal shutters. Now housing the offices of the Virgin Islands Department of Finance, it once served as western headquarters for the French 'Compagnie Transatlantique'.

Less dramatic, but equally distinctive, are two buildings facing each other across Main Street at Raadets Gade (8B and 32 Dronningens Gade). The building to the north is faced with cut stone, while the counterpart is brick masonry with dressed stone quoins and a ground floor archway. Both buildings are severely simple and rely on their proportions and linear quality for effect.

Still other commercial district buildings are illustrated and commented on in the captions. We have only summarized, however, this diverse and fascinating district, providing, we hope, the background needed for hours of enjoyable exploration.

3 Military Structures

Soon after the Danish colonization of St Thomas in 1666, the first fortifications were planned and construction begun. These early inadequate efforts were never completed and the colony was destroyed by freebooters. When the expeditionary force led by Jorgen Iversen returned in 1672, construction of fortifications was a high priority. Construction of Fort Christian started the following year, and this and auxiliary fortifications were sufficient to repel pirates from then on. The British occupied St Thomas twice during the Napoleonic Wars, in 1801 (for 10 months) and again between 1807 and 1815. The conquests were effected with overwhelming shows of force — 23 warships and 4,000 soldiers in 1801 — and without combat. On both occasions the island was returned to Denmark by the British. It seems unlikely that St Thomas would have been invaded by hostile colonial powers had it been less fortified, because it would have been an easy matter for Britain, France, or Spain to send an overwhelming force into Charlotte Amalie harbor at almost any time during the eighteenth or nineteenth centuries. That they chose not to do so can hardly be due to the fortifications or to the small Danish force there. While representing a largely wasted capital investment by the Danish Government and West India Company and presenting parallels with contemporary military-industrial complexes, the fortifications also comprise some of the most interesting and impressive historic structures in the Virgin Islands.

The first colonists had started building a fortification on Smithberg, a hill east of the harbor, now called Bluebeard's. This site was presumably chosen for a medieval-type keep, out of range of ships' cannon of the time, to which the populace could retreat during siege. The need to haul materials to the top of a hill apparently slowed the fort's construction. It was not ready to protect the new colony in 1666, when it was overrun by pirates who helped themselves to supplies and 'borrowed' a ship. The ruins of the Smithberg fort were obliterated by later building.

The site of Fort Christian, on a prominent peninsula in the middle of the harbor, was selected on a very different basis — to return the fire of hostile ships and aggressively defend the colony. This strategy required a

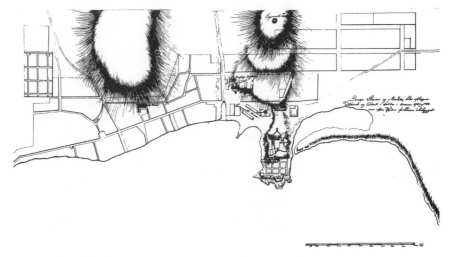

A map by Oxholm
c. 1780 showing the
site of Fort Christian.
Notice the pronounced
peninsula, Government
and Denmark Hills
behind, and the lagoon to
the east. Compare with
the earlier map on page 4
which also shows
Smithberg to the east.

Bluebeard's Castle watch
tower, St Thomas.

much more substantial fort, and the Danish expeditionary force of 1672 was ready to make the necessary investment.

The peninsula on which the fort was built has been largely obscured by subsequent landfills. In the seventeenth century, the shoreline to the west of the fort extended well to the north beyond Emancipation Park. To the east, the shoreline was also further north than it is now, and behind it there was a lagoon which reached Norre Gade. The lagoon's outlet was just east of the fort, and used to have a bridge over it. The site was protected by sea and lagoon on three sides and it commanded most parts of the harbor.

Not only has the peninsula been filled in on both sides of the fort, but Fort Christian itself has changed enormously since the 1670s. The first fort was probably a group of shelters surrounded by a wooden palisade. By 1672, the fort was the seat of government, the governor's residence and

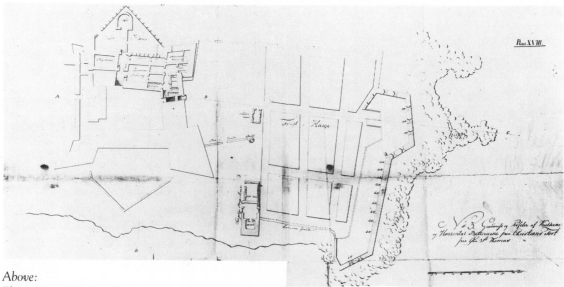

Above:
Plan of Fort Christian, St Thomas, by Oxholm c. 1780.

Right:
Detail of Terreplein Batteries, Fort Christian, from the plan by Oxholm c. 1780.

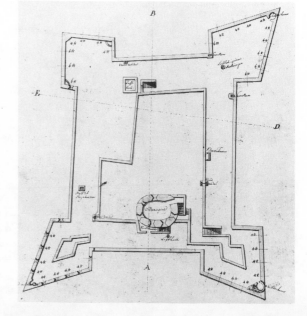

the place of worship. In 1676 a tower within the fort was erected and the outer walls were complete. Late in that year Denmark-Norway entered the war against the French and the fort had to be ready to protect St Thomas from the French, who held several islands in the West Indies, including St Croix. In February 1678, 60 men from St Croix attempted to capture the fort by surprise and failed. The French raided St Thomas and captured a number of blacks and planters who had not sought refuge in the fort, including three free black planters who, with the slaves, were taken to St Croix and sold. Governor Iversen protested and sought the release of these free blacks as late as 1681.

In keeping with seventeenth century military theories, the fort was planned as a rectangular citadel with projecting bastions at each corner. Concessions to the terrain and shortages of labor and time resulted in a very irregular alignment of the walls, and the conventional moat had to be dispensed with. In place of a moat, the area was surrounded by a palisade made of wooden stakes with gates which could be locked. In addition, cacti were cultivated between the palisade and the walls. Within its three- to six-foot-thick walls, Fort Christian had 21 structures. Many of these were built against the outer walls. The largest of the freestanding buildings was the tower, built in 1676, which stood in the northwest corner of the courtyard. This tower was torn down in the late 1870s, when the present Gothic revival clock-tower and north facade were built. Many other major modifications were made to convert Fort Christian into a police station and prison, which it was until the late 1970s. The fort has served every conceivable public function and dozens of buildings have been constructed and later removed within its walls. One was a church, built in 1706 and demolished in 1752, resulting

Gothic revival tower and front added to Fort Christian, St Thomas, in 1878.

in the south side of the courtyard being raised to its present level, and converting the rooms in that area from ground level to basement. In spite of the many changes over the centuries, Fort Christian still retains essential parts of the seventeenth century structure, as well as early eighteenth century additions. Interestingly enough, the fort is the only building in the Virgin Islands which has been in uninterrupted use for more than three centuries, and this in spite of the inadequacy of its facilities by both past and present-day standards.

The fort, while optimally situated to protect the town and harbor, had two important strategic weaknesses in terms of seventeenth and eighteenth century warfare. First, the hills above the town could be captured by an invading force and used to shower the fort with cannon and musket fire (see the map on page 4) and second, hostile ships could enter the harbor, stay out of range of the fort's artillery, and land a force at Long Bay. The first problem was solved by placing small fortified towers on two of these hills. Trygborg, the present Blackbeard's castle, was constructed in the early 1680s and Frederik's Fort, now Bluebeard's Castle, was finished in 1689. A guardhouse was built at the east end of Long Bay to discourage landings. It was abandoned in the early 1700s, its function filled by a guardhouse on Flag Hill, to the southeast, from which approaching ships could be observed and signals sent to Fort Christian. A battery was built on the east side of the harbor entrance, where Frenchman's Reef Hotel now stands. In 1780 Prince Frederik's Battery on Hassel Island was added to guard the west side of the harbor entrance.

*Blackbeard's Castle
watch tower, St Thomas.*

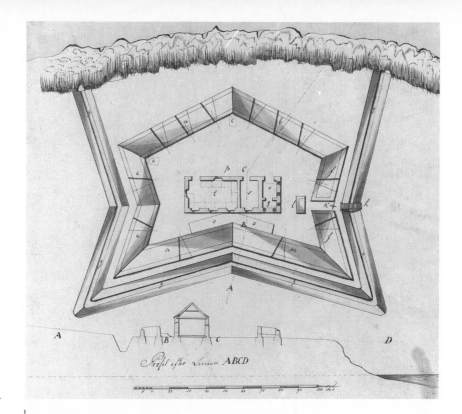

Battery on Pacquereau Point, Estate Bakkeroe, now site of Frenchman's Reef Hotel, St Thomas, by Oxholm c. 1780 (plan and side elevation).

Prince Frederik's battery on Hassel Island.

By the mid-eighteenth century, improvements in artillery rendered Fort Christian and its supporting positions obsolete. When the British occupied the Danish West Indies early in the nineteenth century, they fortified and established their garrison at Cowell and Shippley Batteries on the peninsula (now Hassel Island) on the west side of the harbor — a more suitable defensive position than Fort Christian. This was also the location of the US Navy station in the 1920s and 30s.

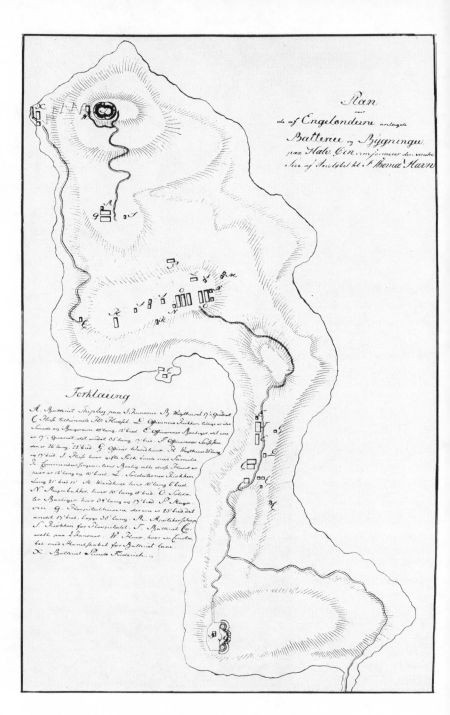

Danish map of British fortifications on Hassel Island, 1802. Shippley Battery is shown at the northern end of the island (bottom), Cowell Battery is on the elevated land at the southern end (top), and Prince Frederik's Battery (marked x) is on the coast immediately below it.

The Danes added the magazine on Hassel Island during the 1840s and in 1874 replaced a two-story wooden barracks south of Fort Christian with the present masonry structure. It is the third barracks building on the same site and a lone survivor of the many structures of Fort Christian that were erected south and east of the fortifications in the eighteenth and nineteenth centuries. Built in a period of eclecticism, it has a vaguely baroque character that does not, however, succeed in hiding the

The Danish magazine on Hassel Island.

Virgin Islands Legislature and former military barracks, south of Fort Christian, St Thomas.

nineteenth century origin of its design. The building is an apple green color with a red roof. The white banding and accents in black and gold on the escutcheons, and cast-iron rails on the grand staircase of the main entrance, alleviate the formality of its design. In addition to serving as a military barracks, it was the Charlotte Amalie High School before it became the seat of the Virgin Islands Legislature.

The US Navy administered the islands after their transfer from Denmark in 1917 until 1931 and there was a substantial military presence on St Thomas until well after World War II. The major installations were the submarine base in Crown Bay and the airfield (now Cyril King Airport), but there were also ammunition dumps, gun emplacements, and other structures at various points along the south coast and on Water Island. Most of the hillside water catchments were built during the Navy administration. That St Thomas had strategic importance as a naval and air base during this period is shown by the fact that the governors were rear admirals until 1922, after which they were captains. We have heard that the United States planned to bring Churchill and his government in exile to the Virgin Islands in case the Nazis overran Britain, but the story may well be apocryphal. Since the Second World War, military presence on St Thomas has been reduced to a missile tracking station on top of Crown Mountain, sailors on shore leave, and recruiting activities. The Navy still has a base at the southeastern tip of Puerto Rico, Roosevelt Roads, and carries out maneuvers around Vieques, which can be seen and heard in the Virgin Islands.

Map of Coral Bay, St John, 1720. The original fort can be seen at the end of the peninsula which extends southwards towards the centre of the map.

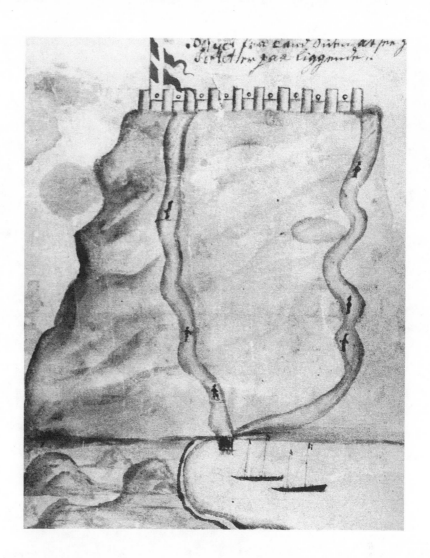

Section of the 1720 map showing the original fort at Coral Bay abandoned after the 1733 slave rebellion.

St John was annexed by the West India Company in 1718 and work on fortifications at Coral Bay, on the east end of the island, was started immediately. A battery of nine or ten cannon was located on the summit of Fortsberg Hill, commanding the entrance of the harbor. The land- or back-side of the fort was an enclosure surrounded by wooden palisades. The slave rebellion mentioned in Chapter 1 started here. It was the first major slave uprising in the West Indies which required multi-national force to repress it. In 1736, while the memory of its horrors was still fresh, Frederik's Fort was constructed on the same site, but in a more substantial manner. It is a rectangular masonry citadel with projecting corner bastions and walls standing 12 to 20 feet above grade; its defenses were now directed inland as well as towards the harbor. A few years later, a coastal battery facing the entrance to Coral Bay was built lower down Fortsberg Hill. A battery was also built to protect Cruz Bay and, as with Frederik's Fort, its defenses were directed inland as well as towards the sea.

Frederik's Fort at Coral Bay, built in 1736.

Battery at Cruz Bay, St John

Public Buildings

Many of the public institutions of St Thomas and St John are housed in historic structures, but few in buildings constructed for the purposes they now serve. There is little older architecture that can be considered to be truly civil-governmental in nature. Many offices, warehouses, and private residences erected in periods of prosperity have been adapted to public purposes as commercial activities have declined and government functions increased.

The tightfisted policies of the West India Company during Charlotte Amalie's first period as capital in 1672–1755, and a declining economy when it again became capital in 1871 to some extent explain the dearth of older civil-governmental buildings on St Thomas and St John. Abolition of some institutions, fires, and other disasters to a lesser degree explain the meager representation of this type of architecture.

During the seventeenth century all government functions were concentrated within Fort Christian. Initially, this was expedient in a small colony with few facilities of any kind. It was maintained well into the eighteenth century, as the Company operated on a marginal basis and then, during easier times, had to catch up. While the government consisted of the four top functionaries of the Company and a handful of individuals representing the planters and traders, the offices within the fort were adequate, if not comfortable. The fort also housed the governor and other top officials, as well as a garrison, and soon the crowded conditions became intolerable. Early governors chafed at the arrangement· and complained about the discomfort, lack of privacy, and unhealthy conditions. The public rooms did not enhance the dignity of the Governor's office.

Company policies were slow to change and government officers learned to get around its rulings. For reasons of health, the size of a growing family, or simply because the means were available, functionaries established their residences in roomier and cooler quarters on the hillside north of the fort and then took their work home with them. The West India Company protested this trend, but did not attempt to enforce its rulings and may even have considered this an economic means of

43

circumventing justified complaints about the fort. This hillside soon became known as Commandant Bakken or Government Hill. It became so officially when the Danish Government bought out the West India Company in 1755 and built substantial quarters for the Vice-Governor, the Government Secretary and Book-keeper, as well as administrative offices on what is now known as Antonio Jarvis Square and the lots to the east of it. Age and neglect necessitated the demolition of the quarters for the Vice-Governor or Commandant, as he was addressed, early in the nineteenth century and the rest of this complex burned down in 1826.

The present Government House on Kongens Gade (King Street) is the fourth official residence and office of the chief executive on Government Hill. Its predecessor on the same site, an 1819 rebuilding and expansion of some earlier structures, had become cramped and was badly in need of repair. The condition was first given official recognition in the spring of 1864 when discussions were initiated in the Colonial Council on a proposal to buy former Governor Berg's house on Denmark Hill, across the valley to the west, as an official residence for the Vice-Governor. The Vice-Governor, who also served as President of the Colonial Council, favored the proposal. He also suggested that the existing Government House, after repairs, be used exclusively for offices and not as a residence. This proposal was rejected on the grounds that Cathrineberg — former Governor Berg's residence — was far from town, and the Colonial Council then approved the erection of a new Government House. Work was started the same year, and after delays caused by the death of the contractor, changes to the design, and squabbles over payments, it was finally completed in September 1867. Master carpenter Richard Bright, the contractor, was a native of St Croix, and the

Drawing of the second Government House, Charlotte Amalie, dated 1819.

Government House,
Charlotte Amalie.

designer, Otto Marstrand, a local merchant. A professional touch was
added by building inspector Major Strandgaard, who had received formal
civil engineering training in the Danish Army. While Government
House may have been a disappointment to the Vice-Governor, it won
general approval from others. Four years after its dedication, Charlotte
Amalie became capital once more, and the building became the official
residence of the Governor.

By its bulk and three-story height, Government House is the most
conspicuous building on Government Hill. Constructed in a buff brick,
it follows an academic classical style as far as the unyielding material
would allow. The corners have quoins of three courses of projecting brick
alternating with single recessed courses. Horizontally the floor levels are
indicated on the exterior by two projecting header courses separated by a
stretcher course. The door and window openings of the first and second
floors have neo-classical hood mouldings with incipient brackets of
two-brick headers. A wide projecting cornice of shaped brick with a

pronounced dentil course below a banded parapet wall completes the masonry decoration.

The marble tiled terrace across the front of the building is approached by a pyramid staircase. The terrace supports a cast-iron porch and a second-story covered balcony with slender, fluted Corinthian columns and iron-work rails in an ornate mid-nineteenth century pattern. The balcony has an ornate cast-iron cornice that echoes the main one on a diminished scale.

The exterior of the building is completely symmetrical and, in spite of the frilly quality of the ironwork, formal and restrained. At present all exterior surfaces are painted white with the exception of the bright red hipped roof. Originally it was more colorful; ironwork, door-and window-frames were white and shutters green, against the yellow buff of the natural brick.

The ground floor contains the executive offices; the second, which opens towards a garden in the rear, the reception rooms; and the third floor, the private quarters of the governor. The public rooms of the first and second floors have been much altered during the 1930s. The original ornate, rococo-revival decor of the reception rooms have been replaced by a blander decorator-concept of what Victorian interiors really should look like, and the first floor murals of Virgin Islands scenes by Danish artist Frederik Visby have been lost. These rooms are still worth inspection; they contain several paintings of both historical and artistic interest, including two by Camille Pizzaro, the French impressionist born on St Thomas, whose childhood home can be seen on Main Street.

The second building east of Government House, on the same side of

Government House reception room, c. 1910.

46

Lieutenant Governor's Office, Charlotte Amalie.

Kongens Gade (King Street), is the Lieutenant Governor's office. Also a three-story building, it has an impressive portico; four Tuscan masonry columns support a complete entablature and a second-story covered balcony with cast-iron columns and railings. This effect is completed with horizontal banding, a large cornice, and hood mouldings over the door and window openings, all with classical revival profiles.

These are the only buildings on Government Hill which were built for public purposes. The others were conceived as residences, although many have housed government offices in the past, and some still do. They are discussed in Chapter 6: Urban Residences.

Early in this century, Bethania on Norre Gade, originally a residence and now housing part of the Lutheran school, was the St Thomas Post Office. A 'new' — now the old — Post Office, completed in 1935, is on J. Antonio Jarvis Square, just to the west of the Grand Hotel. It is a two-story masonry building with arcaded front, banded cornices and corners, and an exterior stairway at the rear. It is of interest as a recent construction which incorporates traditional Virgin Islands architectural expression. While this building is still a post office, most postal functions have been transferred to the main Post Office in Sugar Estate, a

Government Hill, Charlotte Amalie, just after transfer in 1917. Notice the Stars and Stripes flying at Government House.

steel-frame building with a Virgin Islands colonial motif arcade in front, built in the late 1970s, and to a steel-frame warehouse near Frenchtown, in which no elements of local architecture were incorporated.

The former Harbor Master's Office is a two story masonry structure facing the harbor. It dates from the mid-nineteenth century. An impressive staircase and a balcony supported by wrought-iron brackets (both with handsome wrought-iron rails), give it distinction. It is also one of the few buildings facing the waterfront that has retained most of its original character.

In addition to duties, the Customs Service also collected harbor and dockage fees. Of the several buildings that in the eighteenth and nineteenth centuries housed the Customs Service, only the previously mentioned Continental Building has survived. It served as the main offices of Customs but, as with the Harbor Master's Office, it is now occupied by private commercial concerns. At present, Customs has offices in the Federal Building, in two very modest structures on the waterfront and in the airport terminal. The last is a converted World War II aircraft hanger — an impressive steel frame structure that is scheduled for replacement by a more conventional air-terminal design.

St Thomas, unlike most Caribbean islands, did not have a courthouse until the twentieth century. During the eighteenth and nineteenth centuries, courts and council chambers occupied various rented buildings in town at certain times, and different parts of the fort at others. After the transfer from Denmark in 1917, the Territorial Court occupied part of the fort and the Federal District Court the former German-American Hamburg Line Offices on the waterfront. In the early 1970s, the Territorial Court moved to rented quarters in an undistinguished steel-frame building in Barbel Plaza, just east of town on Lover's Lane, and the

District Court relocated to the new Federal Building in 1979.

The jail had been housed in the fort for three centuries — at least a century too long — and was finally moved to a new Criminal Justice Complex in 1982. Both the Federal Building (designed by H. D. Nottingham & Associates and Reed, Torres, Beauchamp, & Marvell) and the Criminal Justice Complex (designed by the local firm of Robert DeJongh & Associates), which are neighbors to the east of the fort and Barracks Yard, incorporate traditional roof lines and articulated framing reminiscent of the banding of earlier architecture.

Government offices occupy rented warehouses, residences, and other buildings in town, former military buildings in Sub Base, and parts of at least three contemporary shopping centers. A government center has been proposed to consolidate offices of various departments and to reduce congestion in Charlotte Amalie, but this project has not progressed beyond preliminary planning.

A hospital was established on St Thomas in 1744 and, as was done in the eighteenth century and earlier, a plantation was set aside, north and east of town, for its sustenance and income. Almost all of Hospital Ground is now within the city limits of Charlotte Amalie. Nothing remains of the original hospital except for the military ward, constructed during the last quarter of the eighteenth century, located north of Kongens Gade on the west side of Smithberg (Bluebeard's Hill), and which is now a private residence.

Adams House, a former military ward, Charlotte Amalie.

Courtyard of the 'old' hospital, Charlotte Amalie.

The existing 'old' hospital in Hospital Ground is a series of single-story buildings of exposed yellow brick and spalled fieldstone masonry, characteristic of late nineteenth century St Thomian construction. They are grouped around a pleasantly landscaped quadrant. To the west is a much larger mid-twentieth century addition. Both are still occupied by the Virgin Islands Department of Health. A completely modern hospital in Sugar Estate was inaugurated in 1983.

5 Churches and Chapels

The Lutheran Church, as the Danish state religion, was present from the first official colonization in 1666. Pastor Slagelse probably had much in common with other colonists — he left Denmark because he had got on the wrong side of church authorities, he yearned for new horizons, and when he arrived he had to clear a plantation of his own to grow provisions. His parish consisted of about 50 Danes. There were also some other Europeans on the island — English, Dutch, and probably French — making a total of fewer than a hundred. These first colonists suffered many hardships and abandoned the settlement in 1668. Pastor Slagelse and other survivors of the first expeditionary force returned to Denmark.

Pastor Slagelse died on his way back to St Thomas with the expedition of 1671. More than eighty others died on that voyage, making burial at sea an almost daily event. Many other seventeenth century colonists died soon after arrival in the West Indies, so weakened were they by the voyage. Then, of course, life on St Thomas was neither easy nor healthy; many died of malaria and other diseases, and serious malnutrition was probably common. One result was the rapid turnaround of Lutheran ministers — 31 for St Thomas during the first century of colonization. Dividing this number into 100 years gives an overestimate of their life expectancy, as there were many periods of several years without a resident minister. Much of the correspondence from the colony to the government in Denmark included urgent requests for a new minister.

During the first decades of colonization, only Lutheran and Calvinist services were permitted. For a few years after 1672 all services were held within the still unfinished Fort Christian and all settlers, regardless of faith, were required to attend. The need to attract colonists from other Caribbean islands led to a pragmatic tolerance of other religions. The Danish state and Lutheran Church soon accepted freedom of conscience and public services by other denominations — an unusually liberal stance for the era. By the mid-1670s, the Dutch and French Reformed Churches built a church on the shoreline a few hundred yards east of the fort, and others were to soon follow. Early in the eighteenth century, the Anglican Church was established to serve English colonists, the Danish

Government supported the Moravians to run slave missions, a Roman Catholic priest was allowed in as a result of diplomatic dealings with the Spanish colony of Puerto Rico, and Sephardic Jews arrived from the Dutch islands and established their synagogue. Along with its geographic position and a generally neutral government, freedom of religion was one of the reasons St Thomas became the emporium and entrepôt of the Eastern Caribbean in the late eighteenth and nineteenth centuries.

Until 1706 there was no Lutheran church building and the congregation met for services in various parts of the fort. Its first church on St Thomas was in the courtyard of the fort, measured 72 by 55 feet, and had 20 glass windows. It was a half-timber structure with a 'roof curved like an arch' and covered with red tiles. In 1754 another church was built outside the fort. When it was destroyed by hurricane 18 years later, the parish moved back into the fort.

The Frederik Lutheran Church was built in the 1780s and dedicated in 1793. This simple Georgian church with arched windows and doors was gutted by fire in 1825 and rebuilt in the following year, when some Gothic revival trim was added. In 1870, the Lutheran Church again lost its roof, this time by hurricane, and was again rebuilt. The original construction was partly financed by an interest free loan from a free-negro parishioner, Jean Reeneaus. In fact, two parishes occupied the church in the early nineteenth century. The same pastor served both the Danish-speaking white parish and a congregation of Dutch Creole-

Frederik Lutheran Church, Charlotte Amalie.

Eighteenth century side gate to the Frederik Lutheran Church.

speaking blacks, both free and unfree. The Lutheran parsons translated the Bible, hymnal, and other liturgical works into Creole and there were parish schools for both congregations. By mid-century slavery had been abolished and English was replacing Creole as the lingua franca of the Virgin Islands, Danish never having been the language of most whites nor of more than a few blacks. The Danish Lutheran parsons were at a disadvantage in these changing times because most neither spoke English fluently nor had liturgical literature in English; the now English-speaking congregations occasionally thought their parson was chanting in Latin! Nor was language the Lutheran clergy's only difficulty. In their ministry to the slaves, their dogmas concerning marriage and legitimacy contradicted the realities of the life forced upon these people and, as the Danish state religion, they could hardly help appearing to support the system.

The Reformation did not start with Martin Luther in the sixteenth century, but with Jan Hus, the Bohemian priest, who was burned at the stake by the Roman Catholic Church in 1415. The Hapsburgs managed to stamp out heresy in Bohemia and Moravia, parts of the Austro-Hungarian Empire from 1620, leaving the sky-line of old Prague cluttered with the steeples of Catholic churches. Hus's followers continued his teaching in what is now western Czechoslovakia until 1722, when they fled persecution to Saxony, now in northern East Germany. Luther had praised the Moravian Brethren as the church which came closest to the teachings of the Apostles and in Saxony the Moravians came under the protection of a Lutheran nobleman, Count von Zinzendorf. On his estate they built their center, Herrnhut, and they converted von Zinzendorf to their faith. Before von Zinzendorf encountered the Moravians, he had decided to dedicate himself to the conversion of heathens about whom no one cared, and he convinced his new friends to join in this mission, which they did, in abstract principle, in 1728. In 1731 von Zinzendorf and a Brother Leupold attended the coronation of King Christian VI of Denmark, where they met Anton, a negro slave from St Thomas, who told them about slaves who were eager to learn about the gospel. In 1732 von Zinzendorf obtained a royal license for the Moravians to establish a mission on St Thomas, where they could preach to the heathens. The first missionaries were chosen by drawing lots, part of Moravian tradition, and arrived on St Thomas in December 1732. Later Moravians also did missionary work among the slaves on St Croix, St John, and other West Indian Islands, and among the Eskimos of Greenland — also a Danish colony.

The early Moravian missionaries on St Thomas worked as craftsmen to support themselves and lived very frugally. They did not convert many slaves, as they could only meet with small groups at night, but the converts they made seem to have been well instructed and dedicated. In 1738 the Moravians on St Thomas acquired a small plantation, a few miles east of Charlotte Amalie, which they named New Herrnhut. Also in 1738, the Moravians were almost driven from St Thomas, because one of the brethren married a free mulatto woman. The couple and Brother Martin, who performed the marriage, were imprisoned and charged with breaking several laws. Rebecca, the mulatto woman, was sentenced to be sold as a slave, the husband was sentenced to life imprisonment, and Brother Martin's fate was not yet determined when Count von Zinzendorf arrived to visit St Thomas. Von Zinzendorf managed to negotiate some kind of agreement with the Governor and the Moravians were freed. This incident was clearly the result of the Moravians' unpopularity with slave owners and it resulted in their increased popularity with the slaves. During his stay on St Thomas, a white mob attacked von Zinzendorf and destroyed the furniture in the mission. The planters' pleas to the government in Copenhagen to stop the Moravians from teaching their harmful doctrines were never successful and, curiously, the Moravians received more official support than did the Lutheran Church. Opposition to the missionaries declined after these incidents.

New Herrnhut is still an active parish. The old church still exists and is well worth visiting. It is a simple building without the usual church accoutrements and is probably typical of early eighteenth century rural architecture on St Thomas. The walls are of very substantial mass masonry, encasing a wood frame anchoring the roof. The many openings are shuttered, but not glazed. The hip roof is steep and the interior has an unusual tray ceiling. New Herrnhut is a unique model for the traditions of Virgin Islands colonial architecture.

Top: New Herrnhut Moravian Church, St Thomas.

Bottom: Interior of the New Herrnhut Moravian Church.

Nisky Moravian Mission, St Thomas, 1959.

Nisky Moravian Mission was established in 1755 to the west of Charlotte Amalie. The complex consists of a manse, church, several smaller secondary buildings, and a cemetery further west. The church and manse dominate the site and their size reflect the mission's success. The present manse was built in the 1820s, and was gutted by fire in the 1960s. It was rebuilt retaining the masonry walls of the first and second stories, as well as the former roofline. Shutters and other woodwork were copied from the original building and the architectural character of the exterior has been carefully preserved. The church is a remodelled version of the mid-nineteenth century replacement of the original. The church was renovated at the same time that the manse was being rebuilt. Its interior areas were drastically altered while the outline and general appearance of the exterior were retained. With their half-hipped roofs and spartan use of ornamentation, both buildings give the effect of well crafted farm buildings, a style appropriate to late eighteenth and early nineteenth century Moravian brethren.

The same simplicity is apparent in the Moravian's first in-town church. Built on Back Street in the late 1840s, it was intended to serve the former slaves who gravitated to town after emancipation in 1848. The building included a school, for the Moravian Church had been given responsibility by the government for implementing the 1834 law providing compulsory education for all Danish West Indians. The building now houses the offices of *The Virgin Islands Daily News*.

By 1882, when the Moravian Memorial Church on Norre Gade was built, the early missionary taste for rural simplicity appears to have been completely replaced by the parishioners' taste for a church as substantial and impressive as those of other denominations. This imposing baroque church is a departure from the style of the St Thomas and St John missions. Consecrated in 1884, it was named to commemorate the 150th anniversary of the Moravians' presence in the colony. The exposed tooled stone finishes, pedimented door and window openings, and rusticated quoins of this building strike an urban note not encountered in any other Moravian building in the Virgin Islands. It was designed by Carl C. Berg, a St Thomian of Danish antecedents and training. In what appears to be almost an architectural jest, a light, open cupola, reminiscent of the early brethren's carpentry, crowns this incongruous behemoth.

The St Thomas (formerly Dutch) Reformed Church is another pretentious nineteenth century structure. Constructed in 1844, it is almost unique in having preserved intact the design and details of the original structure. Built in the classical revival style when this was at its height of popularity, it stands as an imitation Roman temple — with plaster colored and grooved to resemble red sandstone — in marked contrast to the surrounding buildings or to all other structures in the Virgin Islands.

Moravian Memorial Church, Charlotte Amalie.

*Interior of the Moravian
Memorial Church.*

Inside, however, the colonial carpenters had their say. A three-sided
balcony on slender posts surrounds the central auditorium; it is elegantly
curved with a panelled balustrade that reflects, in its divisions, the
rhythm of the posts. The ceiling is sheathed in wide boards and
ornamentation is limited to delicate mouldings. Everything is painted
white, save the beautifully joined mahogany balcony rails and pew trim.
Surprisingly, the Reformed Church is a half-timber structure with
masonry fill between the wood frames. Even the exterior columns were
built with a lumber core covered by masonry. This may have been the
earthquake engineering of the last century; even if this was not the
purpose, it has been the result; the structure appears entirely sound,
while many masonry buildings have been cracked by the Virgin Islands'
frequent tremors.

St Thomas Reformed Church in Charlotte Amalie. Also see the cover picture.

Interior of the Reformed Church.

All Saints Anglican Cathedral is yet another substantial mid-nineteenth century church built in an eclectic style, this time Gothic revival. The exterior style is carried into the interior and there is little to distinguish it from the Gothic revival churches found throughout the West Indies and in other parts of the world. This church has been much altered. At one time its main entrance, now on the east, was from the west; traces of the original doors can still be observed behind the altar. The balconies along the sides of the church have been removed and the walls stripped of their plaster. All Saints used to have a board ceiling and three-sided balcony, an interior arrangement very similar to that of the Reformed Church. The present balcony at the east end of the church dates from the 1920s when the main entrance in the west wall was closed. The cathedral was designed by the local builder and architect George Tucker and much of the construction was performed by volunteer labor from the congregation. The cost of construction was $14,000, which was considered low even then; it is more remarkable considering that in the 1840s St Thomas was at the peak of its nineteenth century prosperity.

The St Thomas Synagogue stands in contrast to the contemporary nineteenth century churches whose structural prominence reflects at least some measure of missionary intent. It is not set off from neighboring

All Saints Anglican Cathedral, Charlotte Amalie.

merchants' houses on Crystal Gade and blends into its surroundings. A series of steps lead up to a portico supported on two brick columns and the pointed-arch doorway that is the main entrance. The interior is square and dominated by four large Ionic columns supporting an architrave of purely classical derivation, which in turn carries a ribbed vault over the central section and the flat ceiling between the central space and the outer walls. The interior walls have been stripped of their plaster to reveal the rubble masonry in the style currently in vogue, but enough remains to show the richness of this curious blend of classical and Gothic revival design. The mahogany pews and other joinery recall the fine furniture once made in the Danish West Indies. The construction of the synagogue exhibits a very unusual feature worth noting: except for the outer masonry walls, it is a wood structure. The large columns are plaster shells hiding wood posts, as are the beams between them. The ribbed vault is plaster-on-lath fastened to the wood braces of an elaborate roof structure. It is raised 8 inches above the projecting cornice and the opening allows the warmer air of the interior to escape into the attic and out through the dormer of the roof, insuring a steady airflow through the interior. The present synagogue was built in 1833 and its full name is 'Beracha Veshalom Vegemilith' (Blessing, Peace, and Acts of Piety). Like practically all of the religious edifices in town, it replaces an earlier place of worship.

St Thomas Synagogue, Charlotte Amalie.

The Roman Catholic Cathedral of St Peter and St Paul on Kronprind-sen Gade in the western section of town was consecrated as a parish church in 1848. It replaces several earlier churches destroyed by fire and one damaged by a hurricane in 1837. The site required the church to be cut into steeply sloping ground to the north and a reorientation of the conventional east-west axis of the service. Like many other St Thomas buildings of this period, its architectural decorations are a mixture of many different stylistic elements, with Gothic revival features dominating. Except for the replacement of the traditional louvered doors and windows and marble facing of the lower sections of the interior walls, the building retains its original appearance. The three naves have plaster-on-wood-lath vaults, and the substantial columns have wood cores, like those of the Reformed Church and Synagogue. The walls, vaults, and columns have a distinctive decorative treatment and a series of murals. Father Leo Servais and Brother Ildephonsus, two Belgian artists, painted them in 1899; they were reputedly made on canvas which was then applied to the walls and vaults.

Roman Catholic Cathedral of St Peter and St Paul in Norre Gade, Charlotte Amalie.

Jewish Cemetery Chapel, Charlotte Amalie.

The chapel in the Jewish Cemetery on the western outskirts of Charlotte Amalie was built in 1837. Like the New Herrnhut Moravian Church, its architectural interest relies entirely on features of its basic form and construction; its character is also very West Indian. This chapel is a small octagonal masonry building with a single Gothic arched opening in each side. The walls are plastered inside and out. The pyramidal roof is metal sheathed and flares out over the walls and eaves with a lesser pitch than the central section, giving it a look of having settled down for good. Inside, the roof structure is exposed and the elaborate and functional bracing of its octagonal shape provides the only decoration in this elegant small building. Incidentally, this chapel's name is 'Beth Hai-haim', meaning 'House of Life'.

Few eighteenth century churches survive on St Thomas and St John because these wood frame buildings were destroyed by the various hurricanes, fires, and earthquakes which ravaged the islands in the nineteenth century. We have grown complacent in our construction in recent decades and it can be predicted that many twentieth century structures will eventually meet violent ends while the well-tested New Herrnhut Church will survive, a persistent monument to the rural work-ethic values of the Moravian brethren who built it.

6 Urban Residences

Charlotte Amalie now stretches far beyond its original boundaries; the town limits were Market Square to the west, Fort Christian to the east, and the lower slopes of the hills immediately to the north. The demarcation between 'town' and 'country' is still very clear. The transition, dating from the mid-1800s, can be seen in Pollyberg and the area around Lionel Roberts Stadium to the north of Smithberg and on the Belgian Road to the south. On its northern side, the town stops at Blackbeard's Castle, Villa Fairview, Villa Santana, and Harbor View, beyond which houses are surrounded by yards and have a more suburban character. The residential area was so confined due to transportation; everyone wanted to live within walking distance of the various conveniences and social opportunities in town, a preference which persisted until the 1950s.

Incidentally, the town is divided into three 'quarters' by two stream beds or guts. King's Quarter is to the east, its western edge is Garden

View of Charlotte Amalie from Bluebeard's Castle in the 1920s. Three streets visible, from left to right, are: Norre Gade with the Moravian Memorial Church slightly obscured by a tree in the foreground; Kongens Gade (King Street) with Government House and the Lieutenant Governor's Office being the two largest buildings in the middle distance; and Dronningens Gade (King's Quarter) leading up Government Hill, to Blackbeard's Castle.

Street and Post Office Alley. The gut marking the western edge of Queen's Quarter — which includes the center of the commercial district and all of Denmark Hill to the north of it — is visible behind the Public Library. All of town to the west of the Public Library is Kronprindsen Quarter. Curiously, both King's Quarter and Queen's Quarter have a Dronningens Gade, Bjerge Gade, and Norre Gade.

In the commercial district, residences and places of business were often combined. A second floor above a warehouse or shop provided the owner with a place to live and a view of the harbor. Purely residential districts developed in a band north of the commercial district and on the sides of Denmark and Government Hills. A harbor view and exposure to prevailing breezes were important considerations best satisfied by elevation and a southerly or easterly aspect — a description of the 'best addresses', where the larger town houses are located. More modest properties are found in the valleys and on the leeward sides of the hills. A noteworthy feature of all of these residential districts is the maze of narrow passages, many with stairs, which dissect them; these permitted the domestics and tradespeople to service the establishment's homes without cluttering up the front entrances.

There are a number of residential buildings facing onto Main Street in the commercial district. Where there have not been drastic alterations, they have these features in common: a ground floor for shops and storage;

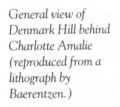

General view of Denmark Hill behind Charlotte Amalie (reproduced from a lithograph by Baerentzen.)

View of Government Hill from the cupola of the Moravian Memorial Church, Charlotte Amalie. The Moron House (center) is flanked by Government House (above left) and the Lieutenant Governor's Office (right).

a usually very small courtyard at the rear, with an exterior staircase to the second floor; a cookhouse, either detached or in an 'L' extending into the courtyard; and a cistern. A few larger lots allowed secondary service buildings, such as slave quarters or stables, towards the rear. These plans allowed intense utilization of valuable land, and were perfected over many years. Several residences in the commercial district extended the living area by balconies towards the street, often with fine and elaborate ironwork, good examples of which can be observed at 2, 10, and 11 Main Street and at 11, 22, and 75 Kronprindsen Gade.

An outstanding example of the town house in the commercial district is the Enid M. Baa Public Library on the north side of Main Street at Gutters Gade. It was built in 1818 by the affluent St Thomas merchant and landowner, Baron von Bretton. The ground floor contained shops and storage, as was common. A vaulted passage led through the center of the building to the courtyard. An elaborate double-wing masonry staircase gave access to an arched and columned gallery across the second floor, the courtyard side of the building, and to the living quarters, between the gallery and the street. An interior masonry staircase led from the center of the second floor gallery to a third story over the middle half of the building, with an arched and columned gallery facing the street and harbor. Both second and third stories had flat masonry roofs,

Enid M. Baa Public Library, former von Bretton House, Charlotte Amalie.

similar to those of Fort Christian and many warehouses, which allowed them to be used as terraces in good weather. The von Bretton house originally had a fourth floor stairtower that served as a widows' walk, suited for close observation of the harbor, the source of the Baron's affluence. The large courtyard still contains its cookhouse, cistern, and servants' quarters; there was also once a stable or carriage house. The von Bretton establishment extended into the block across Back Street or Wimmelskafts Gade. A series of one-story masonry rowhouses, one-room deep, surrounding a central courtyard with communal cookhouse and cistern, housed slaves and laborers. This complex has been converted into shops and, like the library, can be inspected by the public; the rooms at the southern corners have fine interior roof braces.

Bethania, next to the Lutheran Church on Norre Gade, is a residence of the same type. This substantial building served for many years as a post office and is now part of the Lutheran School. Built of masonry in 1827, it replaced an eighteenth century structure destroyed in the 1825–26 fire which razed most of Government Hill. The two-story building has a sculptural quality and it relies on proportions and sparing use of simple and well-detailed decorations for its effect. The symmetrical facade on Norre Gade has three arched gateways. A somewhat larger entrance provides access to a terraced courtyard north of the building and to an impressive double staircase to the second floor. The upper story has seven windows onto the street, with projecting plaster casings, articulated keystones and panelled wooden shutters with louvers on the inside. Plaster banding emphasizes the building's corners, second floor level, and first floor arches. A low parapet wall, above a light and delicately moulded cornice, supports the hipped roof. A small walled courtyard west of Bethania contains another masonry staircase with the curved masonry rails and round newel posts characteristic of Virgin Islands architecture. Towards the street, this courtyard has a low wall which supports a picket fence between capped masonry posts and a central arched gateway below a moulded pediment. In the yard north of Bethania, a series of one-story buildings against the west property-line contained the kitchen, and other services required by a large residence 150 years ago.

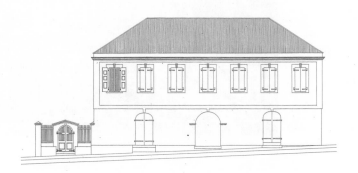

Drawing of Bethania, 6 Norre Gade, Charlotte Amalie (front elevation).

Bethania

*Terraced courtyard
behind Bethania.*

Government Hill was developed as a residential district and, except for the official buildings of Government House, the Lieutenant Governor's office, and the Lutheran Church, the historical structures are residential in character although their present uses vary considerably. The district was planned in the 1760s as a regular grid of parallel and perpendicular streets without consideration of the steep terrain. Although an attempt was made to follow the plan, this could only be done closely in the level land of East Savanne, east of Government Hill. On the hill itself, both east-west and north-south streets had to be laid out in part as extended staircases, which only generally follow the intended alignments. Store Taarne Gade (Greater Tower Street), or the 99 Steps, is an example, as is its proposed parallel, Lille Taarne Gade, which winds its way from Norre Gade up to Kongens Gade and then by more steps up to Dronningens Gade below the brow of the hill.

Quarters B, the westernmost building on the south side of Kongens Gade, was first built in the eighteenth century and was twice rebuilt after destruction by fire. In its present form, dating from 1904, it first served as residence for the Director of the German-American Hamburg Line. The

Store Taarne Gade
(Greater Tower Street)
or 99 Steps, Government
Hill, Charlotte Amalie
(plan and side elevation).

*An early twentieth
century view down
Kongens Gade, with the
Moron House and the
Lieutenant Governor's
Office on the left. Compare
this with the contemporary
photograph on page 76.*

masonry lower story, built no later than the early nineteenth century, faces south, while the wood frame second story is at street level. Simple Ionic columns head fluted pilasters and square pillars which frame the recessed main entrance. The cornice and other decorative features are consistently classical revival. The building's most distinctive feature is the elaborately turned wood staircase in the lobby, which was supposedly removed from one of the early ships of the German-American Hamburg

Quarters B on Kongens Gade, Charlotte Amalie.

Line. Quarters B is now the office of the Virgin Islands Budget Director and the lobby on Kongens Gade is open to the public.

As its name indicates, Hotel 1829, across Kongens Gade from Quarters B, dates from the same rebuilding period as Bethania. Livelier in its architectural expression than most other buildings of its age on Government Hill, it too was originally the residence of a prominent merchant — Lavalette. Built on a very deep lot, the first floor is well above the street level and is reached by a flight of steps. A paved terrace across the entire width of the building supports tall, square, and over-dimensioned masonry pillars with widely projecting collar and cap mouldings; these carry a light second-floor balcony of wood, with delicate iron railings. The courtyard at the back has formalized masonry staircases and the same ornate treatment of large masonry pillars, pilasters, and wall banding. The building's present use has been accommodated by a number of additions; these have been reasonably handled and the original character has survived.

The 1854 yellow-brick building to the west of Hotel 1829 is also partially open to the public. In its material and restrained use of ornamentation, it is representative of many late nineteenth century buildings in Charlotte Amalie. Referred to as the 'Copenhagen style' by the Danish architectural historian Professor Engquist, other excellent

Hotel 1829 on Kongens Gade, Charlotte Amalie.

1854 yellow-brick building on Government Hill, Charlotte Amalie, which is typical of its kind.

Bornn House on the corner of Norre Gade and Lille Taarne Gade, Government Hill, Charlotte Amalie.

Below:
Lutheran parsonage on Lille Taarne Gade, Government Hill, Charlotte Amalie.

examples can be seen on Norre Gade and Hospital Street.

Most other buildings on Government Hill are either still private residences or offices that can only be viewed from the street. Of special interest is the Bornn House, contemporary with Bethania, on the corner of Norre Gade and Lille Taarne Gade. On the same stepped street next to Government House is the Lutheran parsonage, which dates from the mid-eighteenth century; it is the only building in the neighborhood to retain its eighteenth century appearance and is notable for its simplicity. Lille Taarne Gade leads up to Queen Street and the Dutch Reformed parsonage on the uphill side of the street; it is a classical revival house with columned portico built in the 1840s. Crown House, just west of Lille Taarne Gade, is a large wooden structure with a huge half-hipped roof as its most striking feature. The plain exterior of this nineteenth century building belies the real elegance of its interior. It was, for a period, the residence of the illustrious Danish Rothe family that contributed a Governor General of the Danish West Indies, as well as a Commandant of St Thomas, and has many historical associations. Also on Queen Street, farther up the hill and nearer the seventeenth century fortification, Blackbeard's Castle, are two characteristic late nineteenth century residences with elaborate, frilly, cast-iron balconies and stairs, which contrast sharply with the simple lines of the buildings proper.

Crown House, a former residence of the illustrious Rothe family, on Queen Street, Charlotte Amalie.

Returning to Kongens Gade by the 99 Steps, an impressive two-story building in masonry and wood can be observed on the west side. The shingled main floor has quoined corners, alternating triangular and oval segmented pediments on brackets over door and window openings, as

Nineteenth century residence below Blackbeard's Castle watch tower, Charlotte Amalie.

well as other elaborate wood detailing. It dates from the early nineteenth century, but is very reminiscent of eighteenth century buildings on St Croix, and may well express a local builder's desire to recapture a past architectural style.

On Kongens Gade, the 1844 building just west of the Lutheran parsonage was the residence of the Director of the Danish West Indies Bank, established in 1836. Farther east, just below Government House, is the residence of the Moron family, which included prominent merchants of the late 1800s. More recently and until a few years ago it served as the Virgin Islands Government Finance Office, and is a characteristic late 1800s St Thomas masonry town house. Its most conspicuous feature is a wide second-story wood balcony supported by wrought iron 'S' shaped brackets, such as are found throughout town on nineteenth century buildings. This building has an appealing simplicity and it harmonizes well with its more flamboyant neighbors.

Three buildings on Hospital Street, facing the park below Government Hill, illustrate the range of variation found in St Thomas architecture. Constructed in yellow brick, wood, and plastered-rubble masonry respectively, all three were built in the mid-nineteenth century. Although each is completely different in architectural expression, they form a harmonious group. The most elaborate of these residences is on

75

Above:
Moron House, Kongens
Gade, Charlotte Amalie.
The Lieutenant
Governor's Office is
immediately behind it.

Three houses on Hospital
Street which face FDR
Park below Government
Hill, Charlotte Amalie.

*Cast-iron balcony on a
residence just off Bjerge
Gade, Denmark Hill,
Charlotte Amalie.*

the corner of Norre Gade; with its pedimented window openings, pannelled shutters, and other Renaissance revival details, it is as 'High Victorian' as the local taste ever wanted to aspire.

The older residential quarter on the sides of Denmark Hill, north of the commercial district, is completely different in character from Government Hill. The layout of the streets made concessions to the terrain: they wind around the hill, are closer together, and have smaller lots and tighter groupings of buildings. Some of the most attractively landscaped step streets in Charlotte Amalie are to be found in this quarter. While many of the buildings are distinguished architecturally, it is their inter-relationship and the often steep winding streets and alleys which make the total effect of this district particularly charming. This neighborhood was razed by fire three times in the early 1800s; and although it has no buildings that can be dated with confidence, in their present form, to earlier than the nineteenth century, it has preserved an old look.

The Baerentzen House at the head of Queens Cross Street is a two-story, masonry building with highly decorated banding, quoins, and an unusual perforated parapet wall. It is a good example of the new construction in this part of town after the fires of 1825 and 1826. Distinct in character and possibly much older is the Old Unity Lodge on Norre Gade, further up the hill. Acquired by the Masons in 1908, this two-story masonry residence is no longer in use and has deteriorated in recent years. Like the building on the 99 Steps, it has alternating triangular and segmented window pediments and a widely projecting cornice, as well as corner banding, resulting in a baroque appearance. An arcaded forecourt and an imposing masonry staircase leading from its lower level to both the first and second floors of the building add grandeur to this already impressive structure.

Villa Santana, higher up the hill, should be noted for its historical association, if for no other reason. In 1844 the exiled Mexican president Antonio Lopez de Santa Ana, of El Alamo fame, moved here. The building, however, is older, and has only one story, which is unusual for a large St Thomas residence. Unfortunately, it was severely damaged by fire in 1985.

At the same elevation, but on the east side of Denmark Hill, is the

Baerentzen House at the head of Queens Cross Street, Charlotte Amalie.

Baerentzen House (detail).

Gateway to Petit House, Denmark Hill, Charlotte Amalie. Notice the use of brick and tuff.

1870s Petit House, a large two- and three-story masonry structure of field stone with yellow brick banding, quoins, cornice, and window framing. The rubble masonry of the Petit House is spallded with 'blue back', a blue-grey tuff common on the island, and the contrast in color and texture of the materials adds interest to this formal and completely symmetrical building. The combination of materials and the finishing technique are unique to St Thomas and were commonly used in the late nineteenth century; other examples can be observed in Bakery Square on Back Street, the exceptionally fine warehouses of 75 Kronprindsen Gade, as well as in several residences on the western edge of town.

An unusual residence called Fairview should be noted. It is outside the older residential quarters, at the head of the valley between Government and Denmark Hills, on a steeply sloping site. The buildings surround an interior courtyard and are elevated and separated from the street by a massive retaining wall. A marble plaque gives the date of construction as 1848, 5608 in the Jewish calendar, and the Hebrew text of Psalm 127, verse 1: 'Except the Lord build the house, they labour in vain that build it'.

The homes of the workers and artisans who built the grander residences and shouldered the labor of the trade and shipping in the harbor could once be found in all parts of Charlotte Amalie. Their modest size

Plaque at Fairview, Charlotte Amalie.

Typical wood-frame house in Savanne, Charlotte Amalie.

and typically primitive condition have made them more prone to replacement than larger houses, and many have disappeared in recent decades. A number still exist in Savanne, the old free black quarter between Denmark and Frenchman Hills, and in the western extension of town. In their most primitive form they are single-story, one-room deep, two- or three-room long rowhouses, constructed in wood with shingled or clapboard walls, and with a saddle or hipped roof. The shuttered windows and doors may be smaller than those of other buildings, but they are no different in detail and appearance. The exposed studs and rafters often exhibit such refinements as beading, intricate bracing, and other features of fine carpentry. Generally raised well above street level, they have masonry steps supported by arches over the gutters in front of the houses. Where space allowed, they have a porch with shed roof on wood posts. The outhouse and community cistern are largely things of the past and almost all of the small houses still in use have been modernized with interior plumbing.

The better developed types of small house are two rooms deep, with both front and back porches, and a cistern and cook house behind the main building. More prosperous artisans lived in two-story houses in both masonry and wood, with second-story balconies. Except for their size, they do not differ in character and plan from more ambitious residences. All of these types can be seen on a drive through Savanne. In recent years, the stigma of the 'bad years' and the poverty and primitive conditions associated with these modest buildings, in the minds of many people, has begun to wear off, and many have been repaired and sensitively modernized. This can be seen among blander modern replacements in reinforced concrete and unregenerate contemporaries.

7 Plantations

The intent of the Danish West India Company when colonizing St Thomas in the late 1600s was to create a plantation society. The colony was to meet the demands of Scandinavia and the Baltic states for sugar, cotton, tobacco, and other tropical produce so highly valued in Europe. It was for the same purpose that the Company expanded into St John half a century later and that it acquired St Croix in 1733. All three islands were initially developed as agricultural communities.

The first settlers supplemented their modest harvests of tobacco, sugar, and cotton with tropical woods, indigo, and ground provisions (tubers such as yams and manioc). For several decades tobacco was the most important crop and for years rolls of tobacco served as currency. As time passed and more land came under cultivation the main efforts of the planters went into the production of sugar — the most profitable of crops. The success of agro-industry became the gauge by which the economic viability of the colony was measured. Other crops besides sugar — cotton especially, because it could be cultivated in areas too dry for cane — continued to be important. It was sugar, however, which left the most lasting social and architectural legacies.

The production of sugar and its by-products, rum and molasses, was, and still is, a capital and labor-intensive enterprise in the Caribbean. Whereas tobacco, the original West Indian export crop, was often cultivated by individuals or families with small landholdings, sugar required a large labor force of slaves, substantial processing facilities and, to make it a viable operation, more land. The 'works' had to include at least a horsemill with machinery for pressing the cane, a factory with a boiling bench, a still, and curing and storage houses. These basic features were usually supplemented with a 'bagasse' shed (where pressed cane was dried before being used as fuel), shops, oxpounds, stables, cisterns and, where terrain and wind exposure permitted, a windmill tower. All plantations had a 'village', where the slaves lived, and most had a 'great house', their owner's residence. It is the remains of these large and well built facilities that are the most conspicuous reminders of past agricultural activities. Traces exist of the barns, sheds, and storage buildings utilized in the processing of tobacco and cotton, but these were of lighter construction and their remains are less apparent.

St Thomas and St John were brought under cultivation during the early unstable decades of the colony's history. Their mountainous terrain and thin soil did not discourage early settlers, although the plantations proved to be susceptible to droughts and extreme rainfall — both regular occurrences — and intense cultivation in these islands required a disproportionate amount of labor to maintain it. By the mid-1700s, trade centered on St Thomas's harbor, which became a source of revenue rivalling agriculture. Those planters with initiative became merchants and moved to Charlotte Amalie. Their plantations were left to overseers and occasional inspection visits. Plantations continued to be operated into the nineteenth century, not because they were economically viable, but because the status of planter added social distinction and often tax advantages. After 1848, when slavery was abolished in the Danish West Indies, the commercial cultivation of sugar cane and cotton was, to all intents and purposes, over on St Thomas. On St John, with its better soil and lack of other sources of revenue, such agriculture continued for a few more decades.

The commercial development that once was envisioned around the natural harbor of Coral Bay on St John never materialized. For lack of other sources of revenue there was a greater incentive to make the most of the production of the soil. The bloody slave uprising of 1733–34 had put an abrupt halt to the early rapid development of St John. By the 1740s agricultural activities were again expanding and by the late 1780s St John reached a peak of prosperity. Agriculture continued to be pursued more seriously than on St Thomas and sugar production continued there in a modest way into the 1900s. The impressive windmill towers that are such a conspicuous feature of the landscape on St Kitts, St Croix, and other really prosperous sugar islands, can be taken as a measure of the relative intensity that St John and St Thomas brought to bear on agricultural activities. St John, with a considerably smaller land area has five windmill towers as compared to the four on St Thomas. As late as the mid-nineteenth century, two plantations on St John installed steam engines in their factories to improve sugar production, while no such effort was made on St Thomas.

Farm buildings and structures including sugar factories are not highly visible on St Thomas. Some have been preserved in a condition that still gives an idea of their original functions, but these are difficult to reach and on private property. The few that are both accessible and have been preserved have found other uses and conversion has obscured their original character.

Of the four windmill towers, Contant Mill has on occasion been open to the public as part of a restaurant. It is among the most ornamental in the Virgin Islands. The entrance through which the cane stalks were brought to be ground is flanked by pilasters supporting a curved pediment decorated with a flaming urn and an oval marble plaque informing the viewer that the windmill was dedicated by Governor Ernest Friderich von Walterstorff in 1790. The other three St Thomas mills are on private property, but with luck these can be seen among the trees at Fortuna and Solberg to the west of town and Raphune to the east. This latter mill was once owned by the Moravian Mission and has a keystone with the then revolutionary inscription 'LIB ET FRAT 1780'.

Two St Thomas factory sites are open to the public. At Lovendal, now known as Mahogany Run, the restaurant 'The Stone Farmhouse' is in a restored and converted farm building. The second is Jim Tillet's Art Gallery, which has incorporated the remains of Estate Anna's Retreat factory, better known as Tutu. Both sites give an idea of the sound construction that went into these solid structures and exhibit the brick and rubble masonry techniques typical of the Danish West Indies. However, the original building forms and functions are now disguised by overlays of newer work which adapt these structures to their current uses. Both sites also preserve remains of great houses. At Lovendal these are no more than a foundation just northwest of the restaurant. At Tutu, only the lower masonry walls remain of a large wood and masonry building dating from the nineteenth century. Unfortunately, the interior of this house, which was of considerable architectural interest, was destroyed by fire in the 1970s.

Glimpses of other colonial farm buildings can be had from St Thomas's public roads. Half hidden in vegetation, they are not very eye-catching

Remains of the Lovendal factory which now houses 'The Stone Farmhouse' restaurant, St Thomas.

House at Wintberg, St Thomas, which stands on the foundations of a former great house.

and are only a fragment of larger groups of structures. At Wintberg, on the central ridge of the island between Charlotte Amalie and the east end, a wooden house stands on the foundations of a former great house, surrounded by marble terraces. It has a freestanding cookhouse to the northwest of the main building. The site is now a National Park Service housing area. Following the road north toward Mandahl, the horsemill platform, chimney, and factory walls of Wintberg Plantation, now converted into a residence, can also be observed among the trees in the valley below the great house. The same road passes by the retaining walls of the horsemill of Mandahl Plantation, and on the opposite side of the road is the factory site, now occupied by a series of modern school buildings. On the west end of St Thomas, the nineteenth century, one-story great house of Estate Bonne Esperance can be seen from the road. At Bordeaux Bay, on the northwest coast, the ruins of a sugar plantation can be examined.

Surprisingly, given its scarcity of farm buildings, St Thomas has a great

The front steps,
Wintberg

Great house, Estate
Bonne Esperance, St
Thomas.

house which is among the most architecturally ambitious in the Virgin Islands. Cathrineberg, or Denmark Hill as it is popularly known, was built in 1830 by Hans Henrik Berg, a landowner and government official. At the time, Cathrineberg was a plantation on the outskirts of Charlotte Amalie, a location which exempted him from the building tax which applied in town. Only cultivated portions of plantations were taxed, which in this case only applied to four acres of garden out of a total of 170 acres pertaining to the estate. The tax in town, on a comparable structure, would have been more than 20 times higher. Incidentally, Berg and his family of four required an overseer and family and 13

Drawing of Cathrineberg on Denmark Hill, St Thomas (front elevation).

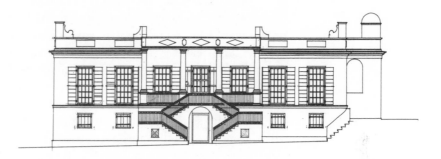

Cathrineberg

servants to maintain Cathrineberg. He also had four plantations on St John; Annaberg, Leinster Bay, Mary Point, and Jossie Gut.

Cathrineberg is sited high above the town and faces east. It is a plastered masonry structure, U-shaped in plan. In true West Indian style, the ground floor, often referred to as the cellar or basement, is of secondary importance, and contained services, storage, and a stable. It is architecturally plain and is treated as a base for the second or main floor. Originally the main access road led up from the east to the impressive double staircase and columned portico that fronts the three center bays of the building. A widely projecting and elaborately moulded cornice is crowned by a panelled parapet wall that at the corners support acroteria of an unusual design. The details are classical revival in character and their execution and application skillful. Although a large building, it is only seven bays wide by five bays deep; the generous scale of its architectural features gives Cathrineberg a grander quality than that generally found in Virgin Islands architecture. Cathrineberg is now the residence of the director of the Danish West India Company and is not usually open to the public.

During the same period of prosperity for St Thomas, other 'country villas' were built on the outskirts of town. Frederiksberg, east of Charlotte Amalie, is now an integral part of Bluebeard's Castle Hotel. In 1818

Frederiksberg, an early nineteenth century residence, now part of Bluebeard's Castle Hotel, St Thomas.

Interior of Frederiksberg.

the colonial government sold the seventeenth century fortification tower with its surrounding lands to a St Thomas merchant and in the 1820s a large residence was built southwest of the tower, incorporating it into its garden plan. Now somewhat obscured by the hotel facilities which have grown up around it, Frederiksberg still gives a touch of architectural elegance to the resort. The columned portico and formal staircase facing the harbor, its east facade and parts of the interior, including the hotel's lobby, have retained the original building's classical revival details.

Similar nineteenth century tax havens have been preserved at Mafolie and Louisenhoj. Both are private residences and not accessible to the public. In the 1930s the New York banker Arthur Fairchild built the present Louisenhoj Castle around the more modest nineteenth century house, and it is this romantic architectural expression that can be viewed from the public roads.

St John, unlike St Thomas, has preserved a fair number of plantation sites with substantial and highly visible remains of their former buildings. Since many of these are within the Virgin Islands National Park they are open to public inspection, and several of the sites are easily accessible. Some have been stabilized and included in the Park Service's very informative interpretative program.

A tour of St John's architectural remains could well start with the Cruz Bay Community Center and Library on the eastern outskirts of the town.

Estate Louisenhoj, St Thomas.

Like other towns in the Virgin Islands, Cruz Bay has expanded well beyond its originally planned boundaries; the library is located in the recently restored Estate Enighed Great House, once outside the town limits. Enighed (Danish for concord) was a sugar plantation and had the usual complement of factory, horsemill, and other structures required for the processing of the cane; these were located at the lower elevation to the west of the great house. Only the great house and an adjoining cemetery have been preserved. The restored great house is a mid-nineteenth century, rubble-masonry building. Although sited on a hill-side sloping down both to the north and west, the builders in true Virgin Islands architectural tradition managed to give the structure a disciplined and orderly look by the regular placement of windows and door openings. A roofed terrace stretches across the western front of the building. Only the impressive dogleg masonry-staircase, that provides access to the terrace and the main entrance of the great house, diverges from the symmetry of its front. The banding in plaster follows a traditional pattern and the pediments over doors and windows, as well as the cornice, are mildly Victorian versions of classical revival moulding details.

Proceeding north from Cruz Bay on the shoreline road the visitor will pass by Caneel Bay Plantation. It was originally called Durloo Plantation and was one of the first to be brought under cultivation after the Danish annexation of St John. During the slave uprising of 1733–34, Caneel Bay Plantation was a refuge for planters from other parts of the island. It was the setting of several pitched battles and the staging area for the recapture of St John.

Caneel Bay Plantation has retained highly visible remains of its sugar factory, horsemill, overseer's residence, and oxpound. The ruins have been stabilized and incorporated in the landscaping of the resort; the oxpound and the mill platform have been adapted to modern uses. All of the buildings are later replacements of the early eighteenth century originals and the factory can be considered an unfinished version of the typical late eighteenth century T-shaped layout. The large mill platform at Caneel Bay now supports a bar and terrace restaurant. It has been covered with an umbrella-like roof reminiscent of the much smaller roofs that often covered the machinery of horsemills.

Further along the Northside Road as one leaves Hawksnest Bay, a short footpath provides access to the windmill tower of Denis Bay Plantation. An elevated masonry duct once carried cane juice from the tower to the factory site visible behind the beach in the valley below; fragments of this duct can be observed south and east of the tower. A large figure of Christ was erected by a recent owner of the estate to the north of the tower; it is known locally as the Christ of the Caribbean and is reputedly a portrait of Dean Acheson, of whom its creator was a devotee. Remains of the Denis Bay Plantation Great House and of several other buildings are not at present open to the public. Entering the next bay, the road passes Trunk Bay Sugar Factory. This ruin of a relatively small factory is

Great house, Estate Enighed, St John.

in very poor condition and for reasons of safety should be viewed from a distance.

Cinnamon, originally Caneel (cinnamon in Danish), Bay is the site of one of the first and most interesting sugar plantations on St John. In addition to a factory and a millround, it has the remains of a bagasse shed, curing house, still, overseer's house, oxpound, gatekeeper's lodge, cemetery, storehouse, and other structures. The great house is on America Hill, to the east. This is one of the plantations which was still under cultivation in the early twentieth century; the owners attempted to grow pineapples and distill bay rum long after the collapse of the sugar industry.

Except for the great house, the buildings of Cinnamon Bay Plantation are strictly utilitarian and have no architectural pretensions. They are of special interest, however, for the factory site plan is of an older type than

Factory ruins at Cinnamon Bay Plantation, St John.

that found at the equally extensive Annaberg Plantation, or at Caneel Bay, Trunk Bay, or Reef Bay plantations. In the late seventeenth and early eighteenth centuries, when the Caribbean sugar industry was still young, there was little uniformity in the buildings or their arrangement at different factory sites. Types and patterns developed and were promulgated in the practical ('how to do it') literature. One of the first rules to be established was to locate the grinding machinery higher than the factory so that the juice would move down under the force of gravity. The desire to minimize carrying distances led to the complete overhaul of the early site plan, in which the boiling benches and the other devices of sugar and rum production were housed in separate buildings, often on the same general level, as at Cinnamon Bay.

To make the factory more compact, a T-shaped plan emerged as the ideal layout and was universally adopted by the mid-eighteenth century. The stem of the 'T' was formed by the boiling house, where the cane juice was reduced to fluid sugar and then crystallized by cooling in shallow pans. The solid sugar was then shovelled into hogsheads (barrels) and transferred to the curing and storage house at the head of the 'T'. Where possible, the fermentation tanks, condensation cisterns, and rum storage and tapping room were on a lower floor under the curing house, and the still, once a freestanding structure, was generally built against the end of the curing section at the head of the 'T'. Cinnamon Bay Plantation, with its nearly square factory and separate structures for curing, storage, and distilling represents an earlier layout.

America Hill, the great house of Cinnamon Bay Plantation is reached by a steep and overgrown path that branches off the main road just east of the factory site. It is a nineteenth century masonry structure, larger but less elaborate than Enighed Great House, and with spectacular views of the surrounding countryside and of Drake's Passage and the Atlantic Ocean. Remains of the cookhouse, servants' quarters, and a gatekeeper's lodge have been preserved and are, characteristically, in individual and separate buildings. All the buildings are in poor condition and should be inspected cautiously.

Annaberg, located on a small hill beside Leinster Bay, is next on our clockwise tour of St John, and is most impressive both for its site and for the size of its buildings. The hilltop has been levelled and enlarged by retaining walls towards the north and east to provide space for a horsemill, a bagasse shed, and a windmill. The very large (for St John), two-story sugar factory is located inland of the horsemill and at a lower level and various other building remains are scattered around the site to the east, north, and west of the factory. The 'slave village' is located on the steep northern slope of the hillside, where a number of masonry foundations of cabins remain; these were of 'wattle and daub' construction, which was common in the Virgin Islands in the seventeenth and eighteenth centuries and was occasionally used in the nineteenth and early twentieth centuries. The windmill tower is the tallest of the five on St John; St Thomas, a larger island only had four, while St Croix, a less

Sugar factory, Annaberg Plantation, St John.

Windmill tower at Annaberg Plantation.

94

mountainous and more populous island had more than 150 towers.

The buildings at Annaberg Plantation were utilitarian and without architectural ornamentation. A feature characteristic of masonry buildings on St John — and at Annaberg more noticeable than elsewhere — is the extensive use of coral blocks around door and window openings and at the corners of buildings. This usage adds an interesting and unusual texture to the masonry. The major impact of the Annaberg ruins derives from the solidity of their construction and their size; one is impressed by contemplating the facilities and labor required to manufacture sugar on a plantation of even modest size. When one surveys the surrounding steep and rocky hillsides on which the cane was grown, this impression intensifies to boggle the imagination. It is small wonder that the slaves revolted and a great wonder that the sugar industry on St John continued as long as it did.

Annaberg Plantation produced cane in the eighteenth century, but the standing building remains received their present form in the early nineteenth century. It does not have a great house, probably because during the late eighteenth and early nineteenth centuries this land was jointly owned with one or more of the adjoining estates to the east and west and usually by absentee landlords. Thomas and Mary Sheen, residents of Frederiksberg, St Thomas, owned Mary Point, Annaberg, and Leinster estates on St John until 1827, when these properties were purchased by Governor Hans Henrik Berg, the builder of Cathrineberg (Denmark Hill), St Thomas.

Annaberg is the eastern terminus of the Northside Road and one must backtrack to continue a clockwise tour of St John. The former cattle farm at Mary Point is a short drive westwards along Leinster Bay. The pleasant but modest great house is still standing, as are several less conspicuous ruins of farm buildings. Between Annaberg and Centerline Road, the factory sites of Wintberg and Frederiksberg plantations can be seen from the public right-of-way. These extensive ruins of once very productive sugar plantations are on private property, and owner's permission should be obtained to explore.

Centerline Road runs along the central ridge of St John, connecting Cruz Bay in the west with Coral Bay in the east. Eastbound, there are spectacular scenic views of Coral Bay, the British Virgin Islands, Fortberg Hill where the slave revolt started in 1733, and the windmill tower of Carolina Plantation in the valley below. A knowledgeable guide will also be able to point out the location of the original plantation, destroyed in the rebellion, as well as the site of the later Carolina Great House, once the grandest on St John.

Centerline Road passes by the Moravian Mission of Emmaus with its church, recently restored manse, cemetery, and new and old schoolhouses. Continuing south and east to the south shore of St John, the road deteriorates and ends at Lameshur Bay and plantation site. In 1780, Lameshur was classed as a cotton plantation, but even then had sugar processing facilities. The factory site is on a slight rise immediately behind the shoreline of Little Lameshur Bay. Its most conspicuous feature is the overseer's house; all that remains is a single-story structure with a wide masonry staircase leading up to a masonry terrace at the level of the present roof. The second floor, which once contained living quarters, is now missing. Early documents refer to a cellar — the surviving ground floor — for storage. This building organization was common throughout the Virgin Islands countryside and is similar to that of more evolved building types found in the towns of Charlotte Amalie, Christiansted, and Frederiksted, where shops often occupied the ground level. In fact, this scheme has survived in contemporary reinforced concrete residential construction, where the main residence is in the second story and the ground level typically contains cisterns, storage, and small apartments; external stairways are another surviving feature, internal ones being almost non-existent in small structures. Returning to Lameshur Plantation, the scant and hardly recognizable remains of the grinding platform and the sugar factory are immediately to the west of the overseer's house; the walls of the latter have been incorporated into a recent animal pound. Of greater interest is the bay oil still, with coppers (boiling pans) in place, just to the north of the overseer's house; it is a testimonial to the tenacity of an earlier generation determined to keep agricultural production alive after the collapse of the sugar industry.

Lameshur Plantation Great House is on the hillside to the north; it is

Lameshur Plantation, St John.

96

now the residence of a National Park Service Ranger. This building was altered so extensively prior to the establishment of the Virgin Islands National Park that it is now nearly impossible to determine what its original appearance might have been. The site conforms to the norm for great houses. It has a cookhouse, still well preserved; the other auxiliary buildings, such as stable, servants' quarters, and outhouses are in ruins.

Returning to Centerline Road — the New Royal Road of two centuries ago — and proceeding westward, our tour of St John skirts the head of Reef Bay valley. The view from the road is deceptive, the valley appearing to lack level bottom land while the slopes of its sides look too steep for cultivation. In fact, Reef Bay was very productive and in the eighteenth century supported four sugar and two cotton plantations. Furthermore, the Reef Bay Plantation produced sugar into the early years of the twentieth century and its factory was the last on St John to go out of production. A path leads down from Centerline Road to the factory site at the shoreline, with a branch to the Amerindian petroglyphs (located below the cascade of an intermittent stream on the west side of the valley), and another branch leading to Reef Bay Great House on the east. We highly recommend a walk down the Reef Bay Trail, especially during the cool early months of the year and with a boat waiting for the return trip — there is no better place in the US Virgin Islands to appreciate nature and history.

Sugar factory, Reef Bay Plantation, St John.

Reef Bay Sugar Factory dates from the early nineteenth century; it was built to replace the eighteenth century Parforce Factory in the center of the valley, when both estates were acquired by John Vetter. Sited on the level land behind the beach is a one-story, originally T-shaped, building with a built-up mill round. In 1869 a steam engine and new cane grinders were installed, and an almost square addition was built against the stem of the 'T' to house the boiler. The factory walls stand to their full height, although the flat brick roof supported by wood beams has collapsed over the older portion. To protect the remains from further deterioration, the National Park Service has placed a modern roof over the building. In addition to the late nineteenth century machinery, the interior still contains the boiling-bench coppers, as well as drip pans and other implements of sugar production. Reef Bay Factory differs from others on St John by having substantial architectural expression. Corners and parapet walls are accented with acroteria and plaster banding, and windows and door openings are finished with slightly projecting bands. The interior of the boiling house still shows traces of the grey, white, and red paints that once decorated this strictly work-oriented room.

Reef Bay Great House is far the most architecturally ambitious plantation building on St John. Presumably it was the model for the architectural details seen in the factory — the acroteria and banding are similar but more elaborate, and the arcade of the covered terraces flanking the building are nearly identical in shape, spacing, and detailing to that of the factory's firing trench. The site still has the remains of a cookhouse, servants' quarters, a stable, and an outhouse which were given the same decorative banding of corners and wall openings as the main building. It also has impressive retaining walls, masonry gate and fence posts, and terracing. Evidently a good deal of thought was given to the formal landscaping of the grounds. The standing great house dates from the early nineteenth century and replaces the much older Parforce great house, the remains of which can still be observed in the cellar of the existing building. Although in very poor condition, this building is still under roof and, except for the collapsed rear portico, all the walls stand to their full height. The mind's eye tends to adapt it for modern use by the simple addition of electricity and power, until the realization dawns that this substantial residence is not now, and apparently never has been, accessible by road. 'Shank's mare' (foot) and horseback were the rule on St John until very recently; even when Alec Waugh visited in 1950, there were no roads and no cars!

Returning to Centerline Road and continuing west towards Cruz Bay, a stop is recommended at Estate Cathrineberg (or Hammer Farm as modern maps name it). The factory site is only a few yards north of the main road and can be reached by car. There are badly deteriorated ruins of a sugar factory and of other plantation buildings. The main point of interest is the windmill tower, which is of peculiar construction. Most mills, as for example Annaberg's, were given the required height by a filled-in base. At Cathrineberg, however, the builders constructed a

Great House, Reef Bay Plantation.

chamber with a central pillar at ground level that supported the second story, where the cane crusher was located. Access to the upper level is by a T-shaped ramp carried on five vaulted chambers. The center vault is a tunnel through the stem of the 'T' that leads into the circular ground floor chamber with its continuous barrel vault. This unusual mill tower has distinctive decorative features such as vault ribs and banded wall openings in red colored plaster.

Between Cathrineberg and Cruz Bay, Centerline Road passes the Adrian factory complex, with its impressive mid-nineteenth century steam engine; Susannaberg, with its eighteenth century mill towers; and the Bethany Moravian Mission, established in 1754. The two former sites are in private hands and not open to the public. Bethany, with its characteristically modest buildings, can be inspected.

8 Style and Contrasts

The eighteenth and nineteenth century buildings of St Thomas and St John are not just a random assortment of buildings which could just as well have been built elsewhere; there is distinction here. Even the most extreme classical and Gothic revival buildings, which contrast with the designs more typical of these islands, incorporate distinctively local stylistic details; the Dutch Reformed and the Anglican Churches are good examples.

Charlotte Amalie, like most communities, was not designed and built as a coherent unit as were, for example, Versailles and Brasilia. Consequently, the distinctive character of her architecture is a composite of many periods and styles. The most distinctive building type in Charlotte Amalie is the long narrow warehouse. There are a number of such buildings, with their interior alleys, in Charlotte Amalie. Warehouses are typical of trading ports around the world, but nowhere in the Caribbean is their architecture better developed than on St Thomas. Presumably local conditions — small harbor, small town, international entrepôt transhipping to many small islands — combined in a unique fashion to produce these utilitarian and attractive structures. The modern adaptation of these warehouses to tourist shopping malls is successful both functionally and aesthetically. The result is a high density shopping and entertainment district which generates the animated atmosphere appropriate to such activities. This central district is perhaps most accurately described as a 'melee', although some detractors, who presumably do not thrive on bargain hunting and busy restaurants, refer to it as a 'casbah' or 'bazaar'.

The typical non-warehouse building in Charlotte Amalie resembles nothing so much as a schoolchild's stick-figure drawing of a house. This is because ornamentation is very restrained or absent — baroque flourishes, which were muted in northern Europe, can be found on buildings on St Croix, but hardly reached St Thomas (or if they did, did not survive the many natural and man-made disasters that have ravaged Charlotte Amalie). Banding, pilasters, and cornices constitute the more 'elaborate' detailing, except, of course, on Gothic and classical revival buildings.

Much of the variety is to be found in roofs. The hip roof is standard, being found on at least three-quarters of the buildings considered. The simpler saddle roof is less common and found mainly on small buildings. Roof spans tend to be longer than elsewhere in the eastern Caribbean; some are very long indeed. Large buildings in the former British colonies often have several smaller roofs, breaking up a long span, presumably because large timbers were unavailable; this is uncommon in the Virgin Islands.

Proportions are an important element in the interest of the more distinguished buildings of St Thomas and St John. There is also a sculptural quality, derived from roofs, elaborate exterior staircases, and the buildings' bulk; this is apparent in free-standing structures such as Nisky manse, and is also evident in town houses such as Bethania.

What features are notably lacking in the eighteenth and nineteenth century architecture of St Thomas and St John? Covered pedestrian arcades, one of the most attractive and practical treatments in hot climates, are rare; the Continental Building and the old Chase Bank building are two examples (closed in in the latter case). This is surprising inasmuch as such arcades are common in the West Indies and elsewhere and they provided extra space on the second story. It should be recalled that Charlotte Amalie was not a planned town and its early growth was influenced more by economic considerations and scarcity of usable land near the harbor, than by building regulations and public amenities. The arcadeless pattern was presumably set by the earliest buildings on the north side of Main Street; even though these early structures barely survived the eighteenth century, their legacy survives in the nineteenth century streetscape.

Another feature common in the tropics, but lacking here, is the roof overhang designed to shade windows and side walls. We suppose that overhangs are rare throughout pre-twentieth century West Indian architecture because they might make roofs more vulnerable to hurricane damage. There are few dormer windows on St Thomas and St John, perhaps for the same reason.

The West Indian islands are varied topographically, they have unique histories, and their cultures are distinct. It is not surprising that their historic buildings provide many contrasts, which we will attempt to briefly summarize. We encourage the traveler to keep looking; do not assume that having seen one old town or great house you have seen them all.

St Croix, usually visible on the horizon to the south of St Thomas and St John, was colonized from St Thomas and is the third island in the group. It might be expected to have a similar culture and architecture. This is not so. For one thing, there are more and grander great houses and factory sites on St Croix, because sugar cane was a bigger and longer-lived crop there. Both St Croix towns, Christiansted and Frederiksted, were planned and laid out in a grid pattern and had very restrictive building codes. The pedestrian arcades, lacking in Charlotte Amalie, are a standard feature here, and one-story houses on St Croix are often fronted by ample covered verandas. Some individual Christiansted buildings are similar to those on St Thomas, but both towns, with their wide and straight and arcaded streets are utterly different.

In general, the larger buildings on other Caribbean islands are more generously ornamented than those on St Thomas and St John and they are also more commonly built of stone or brick. Heraldic devices and other decorations are common in Spanish colonial cities, while decorated pediments, gingerbread, and so forth are more common in the English colonies.

The Danish West Indies and Dutch islands appear to be unique in their sparcity of government buildings, which so dominate the cities and towns elsewhere in the region. Willenstad, Curaçao exhibits a few streetscapes mildly reminiscent of Charlotte Amalie, but in general that town is dominated by Dutch curvilinear gables and dormer pediments. The similarity stems from both having been mercantile, rather than administrative centers.

The military installations built by Spain in San Juan (Puerto Rico) and Santo Domingo (Dominican Republic) dwarf what other countries could put up, but they were not of much use anyway, since most military engagements in the Caribbean were naval. English Harbour, Antigua is an impressive installation; it was of considerable use as the headquarters of the British squadron, of which Nelson was the most famous commander. Its windward position allowed the British ships to have the advantage over all adversaries.

A distinctive feature of the Spanish islands is that there are very few historic buildings outside the towns. The Spanish landlords lived in town houses or in Spain, and left management of the estates to administrators, whose modest dwellings have not survived. The contrast with Jamaica or Barbados, which are peppered with grand or even palatial great houses, is spectacular. Other non-Spanish islands also have great houses, though usually more modest (in eighteenth and nineteenth century terms) in size.

Contemporary architects in the West Indies often incorporate features borrowed from the historic architecture of the region. The most common such adaptation in St Thomas and St John is the semicircular arched door or window opening. This simple shape was hardly characteristic of any one country's or colony's architecture in the nineteenth century, when it was widespread; its use in the late twentieth century however, is uniquely popular in the Virgin Islands. Another such device less commonly seen in contemporary buildings is the tray ceiling, in which the sides follow the inside shape of a hip roof and meet a horizontal ceiling well above the wall top and smaller than the room's floor. This design produces a cooler and more spacious room than does a flat ceiling and is found in an occasional large home.

St Thomas and St John have distinctive historic buildings largely because Charlotte Amalie has been the entrepôt and most cosmopolitan center of the eastern Caribbean for almost three centuries. Charlotte Amalie continues to occupy these positions in the region, but, unfortunately most contemporary construction is prefabricated steel-frame, concrete block, or reinforced concrete, choices made not because we no longer have good taste, but because high style is no longer affordable. Preservation and appreciation are affordable, and it is to these that we must dedicate ourselves.

Glossary

acroterium: Ornament at the angle of a pediment or parapet (also -ion; pl. -ria).

arcade: A series of arches, often fronting a covered passageway.

arch: A curved structure which spans an opening and supports a mass above.

architrave: The lowest of the three elements of a complete entablature.

balustrade: A rail supported by small columns (balusters), hence any low parapet.

baroque: An architectural style using curved and contorted forms, and extravagant ornamentation, typical of seventeenth and eighteenth century Europe.

barrel vault: A semi-cylindrical vault having the same section throughout.

bastion: A structure projecting outward from the main structure of a fortification, commanding the principal walls as well as the foreground.

battery: An emplacement or small fortification where artillery is mounted.

battlement: A parapet consisting of alternating solid parts and open spaces.

bay: A principal compartment of a building's structure, often reflected in external openings or ornamentation.

beading: Small, decorative, semi-circular, moulding shape applied to timbers, traditionally with a special beading plane, now with a router. This is one of several features of Virgin Islands carpentry apparently derived from shipbuilding practice.

capital: The top of a column.

classical revival: Adaptation and use of architectural forms characteristic of ancient Rome and Greece.

Corinthian: One of the orders of classical architecture, characterized by bell-shaped highly ornamented capitals.

cornice: The uppermost, usually prominent member of a wall or facade.

course: A horizontal row of bricks or stones in a wall.
Dentil course — small uniformly spaced projecting rectangular blocks in brick, stone, or wood used in trim and cornices.
Header course — row of bricks with the short side projecting.
Stretcher course — row of bricks with the long side exposed.

entablature: The upper part of a wall or story, usually supported on columns or pilasters, consisting (in classical orders) of architrave, frieze and cornice.

facade: The principal front of a building, which often receives special architectural treatment.

fenestration:	The arrangement of windows.
frieze:	Sculptured or richly ornamented band between the architrave and the cornice.
gable:	The vertical triangular portion of the end of a building.
gingerbread:	Elaborate ornamentation with scroll and cutout woodwork.
Gothic revival:	The nineteenth century reversion to Gothic architectural styles, notably the use of pointed arches, slender columns, ribs and vaults, prevalent in Western Europe between the twelfth and the sixteenth centuries.
groin:	The curved line along which intersecting vaults meet.
half-hipped roof:	A roof which has a steeper slope on the sides than on the ends, so that the hips end in a small triangular gable, the sides of which are the side roofs and the base, the end roof.
half-timbered:	A type of construction in which the openings of a wooden frame are filled with masonry.
hipped roof:	A roof in which the sides and ends have the same slope and meet in hips which joint the ridge ends.
hood moulding:	An ornamental moulding placed over a door or window.
Ionic:	One of the orders of classical architecture, characterized by voluted (spiral or scroll-shaped) capitals.
loggia:	A roofed open gallery which is architecturally integral to a building.
louvers:	Sloping boards set to shed rainwater outward.
keystone:	Wedge shaped stone at the head of an arch.
masonry:	Construction of stone, brick, tile, or cemented aggregates.
'melee':	Creole for fracas, disturbance, or confusion.
newel post:	A vertical post which provides major support for the railing of a staircase.
parapet:	A low wall or similar barrier at the edge of a platform or roof.
pediment:	A decoration, often triangular or curved, over a door, window, or portico.
pier:	A mass of masonry used to strengthen a wall or to support an arch or other superstructure.
pilaster:	An architectural decoration which looks like a flattened column; also an exposed pier treated as a column.
portico:	A covered entrance to a building supported by columns.
quoins:	Pieces of material by which a corner is emphasized, such as raised bricks or oversized stones.
rampart:	An embankment which raises the base from which the walls of fortifications rise.
rusticate:	To apply a rough surface to stonework.
spalled:	Broken.
spalls:	The splinters or chips of rock used to fill in the uneven surface of a masonry wall, hence 'spallded'.
tuff:	A fine-grained volcanic rock.
vault:	An arched masonry structure forming a ceiling or roof.

Additional Reading

Anon., *The Danish West Indies in Old Pictures; Dansk Vestindien i Gamie Billeder*, published privately, 1967

Anon., *Three Towns. Danish West Indian Society*, reprinted by G. Scantryk, Copenhagen, 1980

Bowden, Martyn J., *Hurricane in Paradise: Perception and Reality of the Hurricane Hazard in the Virgin Islands*, Island Resources Foundation, St Thomas, 1974

Boyer, William W., *America's Virgin Islands; A History of Human Rights and Wrongs*, Carolina Academic Press, Durham, North Carolina, 1983

Buisseret, David, *Historic Architecture of the Caribbean*, Heinemann, London, 1980

deJongh, Robert and Frederik Gjessing, *Fort Christian Historic Structures Report*, Department of Conservation and Cultural Affairs, St Thomas, 1982

Dookhan, Isaac, *A History of the Virgin Islands of the United States*, College of the Virgin Islands, St Thomas, 1974

Gosner, Pamela, *Historic Architecture of the U.S. Virgin Islands*, Moore Publishing Company, Durham, North Carolina, 1971

Larsen, Jens, *Virgin Island Story*, Hunlenberg Press, Philadelphia, Pennsylvania, 1980

Lawaetz, Eva, *Black Education in the Danish West Indies from 1732 to 1853; The Pioneering Efforts of the Moravian Brethren*, St Croix Friends of Denmark Society, St Croix, 1980

Parry, J. H. and Philip Sherlock, *A Short History of the West Indies*, 3rd edition, St Martin's Press, New York, 1971

Taylor, Charles E., *Leaflets from the Danish West Indies*, 1888, reprinted by Negro Universities Press, Westport, Connecticut, 1970

Tyson, George F. Jr., *Powder Profits and Privateers; A Documentary History of the Virgin Islands during the Era of the American Revolution*, Bureau of Libraries, Museums, and Archaeological Services, St Thomas, 1977

Varlack, Pearl and Norwell Harrigan, *The Virgins: A Descriptive and Historical Profile*, Caribbean Research Institute, St Thomas, 1977

Westergaard, Valdemar, *The Danish West Indies*, Macmillan, New York, 1917